COUNTRY
MATTERS

written and engraved by
Clare Leighton

LITTLE TOLLER BOOKS

This paperback edition published in 2016 by
Little Toller Books
Lower Dairy, Toller Fratrum, Dorset

First published in 1937 by Victor Gollancz

ISBN 978-1-90821-338-9

Typeset in Monotype Sabon by Little Toller Books
Printed by TJ International, Padstow, Cornwall

All papers used by Little Toller Books
are natural, recyclable products made from
wood grown in sustainable, well-managed forests

A CIP catalogue record for this book is available
from the British Library

1 3 5 7 9 8 6 4 2

CONTENTS

ENGRAVINGS ON WOOD

INTRODUCTION

Kate Adie

COUNTRY MATTERS – once upon a time, we were all busy with country matters – we worked the land, we lived off it, and only gradually, over centuries, did we did we leave for the towns and cities.

We have a sense that the countryside is somewhere in our history, wherever we live now.

Maybe it's a desire to know our roots, or yearning for a – perhaps – slower, gentler way of life. Perhaps it's nostalgia which insists that what has been lost was better, more natural. There's also the urge to paint a chocolate-box picture of Olden Times, usually ignoring mud, damp and terrible dentistry.

My first impression of the countryside was that it was green with large slabs of concrete on it – the view of a small girl peering out of a very small car as we ventured out of a northern industrial town. What should have been all fields and trees was a curious mixture of corrugated iron huts and crumbling, low, brick buildings with broken windows. There was lots of concrete with grass fighting its way through. I was a post-war child, and this was a rural landscape that had been dragooned into service during the war. Air-fields and army camps, runways and storage depots, all ringed with rusting barbed wire and the peeling paint signs saying WD – War Department. Some camps were still in use, and the sight of a tank trundling thunderously past of field of grazing Friesians seemed perfectly natural.

It took years for these remainders of conflict to disappear. Elsewhere in my rural landscape, the skyline was punctured with pit-heaps, some of which glowed ominously at night, as if volcanoes had suddenly arrived in County Durham. Again, several decades later, even these have been levelled, grassed over, blended in, as if the entire coal-mining life had never existed here. The valleys running up into the high Pennines were beautiful but the villages strung along the narrow roads were grey and quiet. Abandoned cottages were common, new buildings almost unknown. My great step-aunt's kitchen range and privy made an unforgettable impression on a five-year-old. I was a townie and had much to learn. I hope that I have learned that the countryside absorbs change, sometimes shrugs it off, sometimes benefits from it. What is more subtle is the life lived in such places. Whatever draws us to countryside life many years ago, our imaginings are sharpened and enriched by the descriptions of a Buckinghamshire village in the 1930s by Clare Leighton.

Bold and arresting woodcuts show us her world through the eyes of an artist. Her words are those of a woman immersed in the beauty of the seasons and she expresses a profound belief in the importance of the relationship between people and the work that connects them to their surroundings

Leighton was fascinated by the world of rural work. On her travels, she made woodcuts of Corsican washerwomen and clam diggers in Cape Cod. In English village life, she saw a cavalcade of activities which intrigued and inspired her.

One or two of the older villagers she saw in her village just might have been registered in the census of 1851 – the first official acknowledgement that the Industrial Revolution had tipped the centuries-old balance between urban and country folk. The towns promised more jobs, more money, and even though the work may have been in filthy and dangerous factories and mills, we tend to forget that the countryside could be a harsh and unforgiving employer, with tumbledown cottages and capricious weather. And well into the twentieth century, imperial power brought cheap food from around the world, depressing our own agriculture. So much so, that just before World War I, the historian Mark Bonham-Carter wrote that 'the heart had gone out of the village as an economic unit.'

Leighton watches men born into these times, as they sit companionably in the pub or keep an eye on the local cricket match. They have lived through an era when not only the town had become king, but the countryside had had seen its tentacles spread deep into their rural territory. Urban sprawl was on the march. 'Ribbon development' and 'suburbanisation' had crept into the language, and to many they were seen as greater threats than floods or poor harvests. Victorian England was alive to these concerns, but it took time before it was realised that it was not enough to rely on landowners and individual parishes, and that this was a national concern which needed some kind of planning.

Leighton is no sentimentalist, and definitely not in the tradition of Victorian painters and photographers who rejoiced in the twee and the quaint. She doesn't oppose change, and she is writing in the 1930s, when the great efforts were being made to protect what had been cherished for centuries in the countryside. Conservation campaigns, new planning laws to prohibit unbridled development, the importance of the rural landscape to every citizen; these were lively issues throughout the decade. She accepts the signs of visible change – the noisy traffic on the lanes bringing visitors, the young men gathered in awe round the latest tractor at the country fair – but she desires to describe something much deeper than the impact of progress. She wants to express the delight to be had in the unchanging wonder of starlight in the dark woods, the satisfaction of working the earth, the joy to be had in the fruits of the earth.

She wants to emphasise the very essence of living close to nature. What she cares about is what she notices in the gentle round of everyday life. The scene in the local pub is a good example. The men gather there, often to sit without much conversation, drawing contentment from the place, the company and the sense of shared experience. She has, however, no sentimental view of human nature, seeing the unrequited love and remembered disappointment sparked in villagers by the seductive glamour of the touring fair. She notices the spiky differences in status exposed by the Horse Show, and the grumbles about everything from church to ploughing match that 'it's not like it used to be.'

She sees, though, something stronger beneath the surface of everyday comment. Her countryside, she feels, has a rhythm of life that is timeless. The theme of a shared village life holds strong. 'An enduring world' she calls it.

Her woodcuts reflect that strength of feeling. They convey the physical effort of work, the flow of the landscape. They are statements, sharp and detailed, which catch a moment, drawing you in.

All through her writing is the sense that what she is describing is a link in her 'enduring world'. She is writing about villagers who connect to mid-Victorian England, when their village had men whose varied skills were essential, from plough to forge. She sees them in the 1930s, understands that the young men enthralled by the latest tractor are also essential to the survival of the community. We read about this more than another eighty years on. Today there are worries still, about the pressure on the countryside, the increase in weekend cottages, the decline in rural services, the demands that industry should quarry, frack and build. Take heart. Look for the enduring world. Read of an enduring world where success, career, fame, money-making, celebrity are of little consequence. Where great lives can be lived next to nature, seeing the stars, having friendships, falling in love, and finding delight in the practical and the everyday, knowing that the countryside matters.

Kate Adie
Cerne Abbas, 2016

PREFACE

Claire Leighton

I WAS DISCUSSING THE WRITING OF THIS BOOK with a friend. 'I suppose it will be a sort of obituary,' she said. 'Everything romantic in the countryside is about finished and done with. All I can say is that it's a good thing you've written it down before it is forgotten.'

But I rebelled. I do not mean this book to be in any way an obituary. It shall be the record of an enduring world – a world that is as alive and romantic today as it was in the times before mechanisation. Romance need not live only under thatched eaves, drawing its water from moss-covered wells. It can survive the invasion of the tractor and the radio. It feeds upon an attitude of mind, and despite all modern inventions and conveniences, this attitude of mind persists. For the countryman is still close to the earth. I remember one day talking to my gardener about the weather. We craved rain for the plants, but still the skies remained blue and cloudless. 'And yet,' I remarked to him, 'and yet the radio last evening said we were sure to have rain today.' He looked up at me whimsically and with a trace of pity as he answered: 'But be you thinking as how it's the radio that gives us the weather? I tell you it bain't. It be our Heavenly Father what sends it.' This creature of the earth, for all the science that surrounded him, had retained the beliefs of his forefathers.

In the countryside today there is a piquant merging of the new into the old. Horse plough and tractor turn the clods in the same field on the day of the ploughing match. So, too, does radio supply the music at the village flower show, and an electric organ blare forth at the village fair. It may be that the tunes mechanically played are transatlantic, drawn from a world remote from the English villager. But the flower show and the fair persist, while the labouring man who exhibits his dahlias and the young girl who dreams on the merry-go-round upon the village green are unchanged. They are kinsfolk of the Wessex peasant immortalised by Thomas Hardy, and vary from him only in the minor details of dialect and custom. When one considers the enormous social and economic changes of the past twenty or thirty years, it is interesting that there should be so little alteration in the heart of the peasant. Town life has encroached upon the countryside, smashing its isolation with the automobile and bringing to remote cottages an urban standard of living; but there is no break in the beauty and romance of the village. To balance the restless tug of modern civilisation there stand the hills and the woods by day and the smokeless starlight by night. The tempo of life is determined by the tread of the horse at plough or the amble of the grazing cow.

If I am defiant in my defence of the countryside it is because I know it to be the last hope for sanity. Here, in the heart of the labouring man, is the strong sane humour of the earth, without which there is no health. At no time has this been more needed, and at no time have we stood a greater risk of losing it. For with the modern rush of consciousness about the country we may destroy the thing we love. A sentimentalised, self-conscious countryside, fixed for the sightseer, would have lost all that made it desirable. It is the worker on the earth who matters – the blacksmith at his anvil, the shepherd, the feller of trees. From him we must learn.

For my American readers I would say that I have tried to generalise about my countryside. It would be easy to concentrate on those little quaintnesses that mark the English setting, supposing them to have an especial appeal. Living as I do in Buckinghamshire, I must naturally talk of my own people and place them against the background of my own Chiltern Hills. But it seems to me that there are few little differences among the workers on the land, whether they dwell in an English village, or gather the olives of a Mediterranean island, or till the red earth of Georgia. They work and play and love with the same dignity and the same humour, and it is these that I have tried to capture. Into this fussed and restless world they bring the quiet of the hills and the simplicity of elemental thought.

Clare Leighton
Monks' Risborough, 1937

TRAMPS

YOU SEE HIM AT NIGHTFALL, walking the road on the outskirts of a town. He seems especially to come into existence at sundown, as though he were a bat or moth or a clumsy brown maybug. The country road to him is nothing but the space between town and town. He is the 'soft' tramp, who plans his life that he can arrive each night at a different workhouse. This kind walks with determined step, conscious of a fixed destination. His head may droop with fatigue, but his eyes are straight before him, never pausing to look at ditch or lane, or to search for sticks that he may make a fire for his billy can. In the particular rhythm of his walk we can sense the length of white road gathered up behind him, the ribbon of white road lying before him. He is a figure of monotony made manifest. Place him against an incongruous background and you would yet know by the shape of his walk that he was a tramp. His feet have grown accustomed to the smoothness of civilised roads, so that though he may move always with the stride of the countryman, yet there is about him none of the clumsy lurch of the ploughman, with his purposeful plodding upon heavy ploughland.

But there is another kind of tramp, and this is the true one. Not for him is the workhouse at night, with unending trudge from town to town. He sleeps anywhere. For are there not ditches to be found all along his path? Or barns? Or haystacks? And what does time matter, or distance, or weather? It is he who meanders more in his walk, looking to right and left of him, pausing, searching. It is he who is the carefree romantic, and as true to type as if he existed between the pages of a book. And I know for a certainty that he does exist in real life, for I have seen him often and I have even been friends with him.

When he is met on the road, it will be noticed that he travels less light than his brother, the 'soft' tramp, for he has to carry around with him pans and pots, rags for his pillow and knife for his bread. I knew one who even boasted of a razor and piece of looking-glass and changes of shirt. But he was a super-tramp.

There is a small lane in the Chilterns at the bottom of which he can often be seen, lying asleep on his back or lolling against a broken gate. As one passes along the high road one notices a thin spire of smoke rising from the bush tops; he is cooking his dinner. His fire is made from odd sticks and from loosened parts of the little footbridge that spans the Misbourne; for the narrow planks of this footbridge grow fewer and fewer as his visits to the neighbourhood are repeated.

But let us follow our tramp as he saunters along the road. His body is bent under the unwieldy weight of all his worldly goods, contained in numerous sacks thrown over his back. The uppers of his shoes burst apart from the soles, exposing frayed scraps of discoloured socks. His clothing is of a lovely harmony of muted tones; there is no discord to be seen anywhere. The general colour of his apparel is that of the countryside through which he passes: warm crimson-brown of the sun on the ploughed fields, buff of decaying vegetation in the autumn, deep blackish-green of the shadow on a pond under heavy trees. If he is wearing a blatant pink or red muffler, it seems, against the harmony of its background, to be a bright flower in the hedgerow.

It is his head, though, that arrests one's attention. Did ever the beard

of an ancient god curl and wave and toss in the wind as does the beard of our tramp? It gives to him, be he ever so young, a dignity that commands respect. Into our minds come visions of Druidical priests, in their rightful setting of oak tree and glade. Speak to him, and you will probably find that he is far from having the mind of an ancient god or a Stonehenge priest, but look at his head and you are bound to feel reverence, though his mighty appearance be due merely to the absence of a razor. A rush of gratitude warms one that there should still be these wild-faced, grand-looking men walking our standardised world.

Perhaps this gratitude we feel shows when we meet him, for, be he begging hot water or old clothes, he does so always with an innately proud look on his face. He never cringes, or apologises for his dirt or his rags; rather does he give one the feeling that his is the correct method of attire. One might be inclined to think that this pride was due to complete freedom from the embarrassment of possessions, were it not that it is only the men who are independent of pity. The tramp woman, with no glory of tossing beard to cover her poverty, is always a drab, pathetic object. The vision of a tired, pregnant tramp woman who begged at my door took months to dim. Only once did I come across a happy one. She was a Scotswoman, tramping through England from her own country, carrying nothing but a small basket with two divisions; one, she said, for the mind, and the other for the body. In the one she kept her own poems that she peddled, and in the other the food that she managed to beg. There was a beautiful peace in her face.

I knew an old lady who lived far out in the country by herself, beyond sight or call of neighbours. The nearest village felt it as a weighty responsibility.

Supposing she were murdered one night by a tramp: there were so many
of them about. But the old lady laughed. It was true that there were so
many of them about – more, perhaps, than even the village knew of. They
would make a special point of diverging up her lane, asking for boiling
water for their drink. With scriptural generosity she would give them tea
and milk and sugar, butter on their bread, the use of her oil stove for their
cooking. 'And why should they want to murder me?' she would ask. 'We
understand each other so well. It just happens that it's I who have the tea
and the butter. But it might just as well happen the other way round.'

It is a pity that this fear has grown around the idea of the tramp, for
there is much to learn from him. Who else demonstrates the needlessness
of possessions? Who else corrects the blind rush of modern life? There is
dignity in his poverty. He rarely trades on the rags he wears. If he shows
us his worn-out shoes, and asks for our cast-offs, it is in a spirit of the
communism of property. And his laziness? Should we blame him for this?
His attitude to life must needs be based on different values from ours in
that he has none of the usual urge to accumulate possessions. What, then,
is there to prevent him from pausing and tasting life with gaiety?

The gayest tramp that ever I saw was an old soldier who zigzagged
up our lane one May morning. We were walking round the garden when

 suddenly we heard singing. I had
thought at first that it was the chorus
of some popular song. I then realised
that it was not the tonic scale, but
some strange mode closely akin to
plain song, or to the Lydian mode
of the working songs of the peasants
of the Mediterranean. As the sounds
came nearer they shaped themselves
here and there into words, and I heard
with amazement such unromantic
phrases as 'a bit of fat bacon – yes, a
bit of fat bacon.' I listened, while the

voice wailed its disappointment at some unknown person who had 'no good nature in him, and wouldn't give me a bit of fat bacon.' Suddenly I knew that I was present at the birth of a spiritual. Here was the true root of song. And I remembered a story that had been told me of the Southern States of America. My friend had been forced to leave his plantation, and had the painful duty of dismissing his servants. Soon after he had told the head man, he was walking in his fields when he heard voices. He saw there the old servant, sharing his troubles with the rest of the workers. 'Massa's gwan to leave us now,' moaned the old man. 'Massa's gwan to leave us now,' moaned the group. The moans grew and swelled instinctively and unconsciously the quarter tones entered, the phrase was repeated in part and in whole, till the bodies swayed to the rhythm of a despairing spiritual. It was in this way that the song about the bit of fat bacon was forming.

I looked over the hedge and saw a figure so wild that I thought it the product of my imagination. But no, there it was, reeling across the road from side to side, as it climbed the hill. I called to it, and as it turned I saw a face as wild as the figure, with a nose sticking grotesquely far out and a fierce, short red beard. I asked the creature if he would like something to eat, and he came into the garden and sat down while breakfast was prepared for him. And as he waited he talked, and by the time the breakfast was ready I had learnt much about him.

He had been a soldier in the Royal Engineers, and until the rheumatism had attacked him he could have knocked me down, he was so strong. But seeing that he didn't like mixing at night with common low tramps, he always slept in a shed or barn, and of course you *did* get rheumatism that way. It was these winds that got at one. Even the night before, there had been sharp frost and wind, and the straw on the ground had been frozen and had ripped open his trousers all down one leg. It was astonishing what strength there was in frozen straw. I offered him a needle and cotton, but he waved it regally aside: somebody would soon give him a new pair of trousers, he said.

'You see,' he boasted, 'being so used all my life to real good people, I'm bound to come across them still.'

I hated to think of him at night with the cold darting in through these ripped trousers, and begged a pair of long woollen under-drawers from a male member of the household. But my tramp refused them.

'Why, what do I want with them now, with the summer coming on? I like to feel the wind in my legs. Don't you go worrying about me, I'm all right.'

We moved then to deeper topics, and I asked him if he enjoyed life. He braced himself.

'Oh, I'm alright. You see, I don't think. Now, if you took it to heart, you'd die in a day. But I know better. I've seen soldiers what took things to heart and went off their heads. I've learnt my lesson. Not but what I'm happy in the country. I can sing there.'

And then he grew tender and leaned towards me.

'I've been waiting for this, you know,' he said. 'A long while back I picked up a book, and I've got it here, and it may be as it's a good book, and I've wanted to give it to somebody as would want it, and I'd like to give it to you.'

Out from his filthy sack came a newspaper package, and as I undid it, there was *Aurora Leigh*.

'It must be beautiful to be a scholar,' he went on. 'Now as for me, I'm not much of a scholar. While others have been at that I've been building bridges and pontoons all over the world – India, and Egypt, and I forget where. You can't get time in this world for everything. You've got to pick and choose. And if it hadn't been for the drink, there's no telling where I mightn't have been now. But the drink always undid me.'

He got restless, and would move on. He aimed at reaching the West Country soon, and would then wheel round and come back by way of Surrey. Warmed by his friendliness, I wanted to give him something. But he had such dignity in his bearing that I found it hard. All I managed was to offer him the price of a glass of beer.

'Now, now,' he said, as he pocketed my sixpence, 'you don't need to be doing that sort of thing. I expect you're poor like me, if you're an artist.'

When I look at my copy of *Aurora Leigh*, printed in New York in 1890 and inscribed 'With great love to Jimmy from Jessie, 1891,' I see a sack-laden figure in a brown overcoat, purple with the bloom of age, rolling up the lane to the hills. In one hand he swishes a stick, in the other he carefully carries a billy can full of tea – tea with milk in it, to make you strong, for tea without milk never does no one any good! – to be drunk at leisure in the woods. I listen for his song, but it has not yet formed. When it is born, I like to think that it will be less mournful than the dirge about the bit of fat bacon. I like to believe that I have begotten a happy song.

And then I remember a completely different tramp. He was as strange a figure as any, but in place of the usual sly or childish look, he burnt with the fire of religious mania. He stopped me one day in the folds of the hills, barring my path with his brandished stick. The sun caught the sharp planes of his face, throwing into deep shadow the lower part of his bony cheeks. Everything about him, from long pointed finger to pennant of torn overcoat, looked like black lightning.

'Have you ever met a prophet?' His words were the inevitable thunder.

'…A prophet,' echoed from the beech wood slopes behind me.

'Then I tell you that you have today met one. The Lord has given me a message for you – and for you alone.'

'…You alone,' declared the beech wood slope.

The storm of his religious passion played around him. I dared not move. In the stillness of the hills his message rolled and tumbled and roared, tossed back by echo, till sentences overlapped and gained doubled force.

'Listen to me! If you have any genius in you, let it come out. The Lord wants you to speak. The Lord wants you to have courage. The world is full of genius, but the world lacks courage.'

He dumped his baggage on to the turf and flung his legs and arms apart, like a violent scarecrow.

'Now I am a prophet. I am neither better nor worse than all the prophets – Isaiah, Jeremiah, Ezekiel, St. Paul, we are all one.' He shouted his words to a flock of crows overhead. 'When I lie down at night I hear the angels singing and the golden trumpets blowing, and I see the stars above dancing with joy, and God on His throne on high. The day will come when I shall stand before the people of the world and I shall lift up my arms to Heaven and cry: 'Peace be still!'

As he bellowed these last words, a frightened rabbit scuttled across the clearing. Birds in the undergrowth flew noisily into safety.

'And then you will see the Lord coming with glory and power. Even so. Amen.'

'And when will that day be?'

But the prophet had finished. He stooped and packed his baggages about his scraggy person, and turned to leave me. He had delivered his message.

As he turned, though, an idea came to him. He clutched at my hand and held it tight. Uncomfortable electric force poured into me from those spiky gnarled fingers. I almost feared lest I had caught his madness.

'And now,' he said as he moved off, 'now you'll never be the same again. To the end of your days you will remember that you have been chosen – yes, chosen to clasp the hand of a prophet.'

A disturbing quietness lay upon hills and woods when he had left me.

But my special tramp friend was a much less frightening creature. I never

knew his name, and now I never shall, for I think he must have died in one of the many ditches or old barns that were his resting places at night. He would visit Aunt Sarah and me once every three years, as he reached Berkshire in his trudge round England.

I remember the first time he called, an incredibly unkempt figure with a fierce moustache and thick white eyebrows. He was evidently in the mood for a long talk, as is usual with those who live alone. Aunt Sarah and I quickly realised that he meant to spend the morning with us, and as quickly resigned ourselves. He had in him a strange mixture of superb self-assurance and humility. Like a child, he failed to see how we should not be interested in everything that concerned him.

'Come along outside and see my kit,' he insisted. 'It's a large lot to carry, isn't it? But I need all sorts of things for when I am settled. I've a frying pan to cook in and a kettledrum, and lots and lots of shirts. And when I want a change and a wash – well, I take off my shirt, and I have heaps of soap and some soda; and there's always a pond. And when the sun shines, my shirt dries lovely on the hedge tops. And there's my bit of mirror to shave myself with. There's them what makes themselves a sight to look upon in order to get pity, but I says they're not even worth the pity. One should always be fit to see and be seen.' He had the power of transforming his filthy old mackintosh into regal robes, so that Aunt Sarah and I even felt apologetic about our own clothes.

He told us, always without rancour, of his adventures with gamekeepers and policemen. Ingenuously, he had tried to convince a gamekeeper of the economic fallacy of spending one pound on rearing a bird that only costs about eighteen pence when it is dead. But he had failed.

'There's some chaps you can tell a good way off. If they look at you, you know they're alright. If they look aside, they've got nothing for you. But there's some that will even turn at sight of you and walk away when they see you coming. When you come to think of it, it all depends upon if they've got a bottom in them. There's them what's like tailors' thimbles, with no bottom to them at all. And I tell you what it really is.' Here he leant forward, as if to tell us one of the world's secrets. 'It all amounts to

this – if you've got a bit of nature in you you're alright.'

He had left his baggage in the garden, and had come back to the house and was sitting in the kitchen, waiting for us to prepare a meal for him. It was disarming to find how completely he took our goodness for granted. He never doubted that I should get him his breakfast. He had, I suppose, decided that we possessed that 'bit of nature.' He did not ask for the food. He sat down and waited for it. And it came.

I teased him about it, but secretly I was envious of this trust. It made me realise the power of fearlessness. He started again on his rambling talk.

'Why, I've had good luck and bad luck. But things go right and things go wrong, and so I mixes them all up together. If it's bad today it'll be right tomorrow.'

There was a pause in his flow of talk as he stirred his tea. But I was greedy to know more of what he thought and felt and I asked him if he were happy.

'Happy? Why, of course I'm happy. I'm close on seventy and I've worked since I was seven. Three-and-sixpence a week, and seven days a week to earn it in, and two miles to walk to one's work, and on a Saturday a whole big three-and-sixpence.'

He seemed to have no feeling that life had been hard, no atom of bitterness in him anywhere.

'Why aren't people happy?' he went on. 'It's because they worry. I never worry about what's going to happen and everything blows over and one's alright again. All these people with *things*, they worry about how much more they're going to get; and the one thing they don't get is happiness. You can't carry your goods to Heaven. They're no use to you there. But you can take your nature with you – yes, and your gentleness and all.'

He spoke so simply that things that might have sounded trite seemed important. I remembered hearing something like this before, and suddenly saw yet another solitary. This time it was Ted Lawrence, the seventy-year-old thresher who had lived alone all his life in the vale near Shaftesbury. With the philosophy that comes of solitude and mental leisure, he, too, had scoffed at possessions.

'What do we be wanting with money, you and I?' he had asked me. 'They dukes what have so much money, they don't be half as happy as I.' And I had felt honoured to be considered of his company, and sat by him and listened as he sang old Dorset songs and podded his beans.

Yet another philosopher I knew was a little glove maker who lived alone in a mountain village of the French Alps. She sat her life away outside her cottage door, surrounded by her plants as she stitched the ornamental backs to gloves. She had never married, and was alone in the world; but she had a secret that one day, in a moment of unexpected tenderness, she confided to me: she wrote poems. And then she recited these poems to me, sentimental views on life and love and death and flowers and pain and joy. In her lonely dream world she was a richer creature than her neighbours, whose thoughts were only for the housekeeping of the day. In her solitude there was little about her that passed unnoticed. She had time for enjoyment.

'And it's queer,' she said to me one day as we watched a Dauphiny sunset flinging its golden clouds across the valley, 'it's queer, but all the loveliest things in the world are to be had for nothing.'

I fell to thinking of the truth in her words, remembering the beauty of the sudden sight of an entire village threshing, as I had turned a corner in a mountain road near her home. Surely no purchased loveliness could equal that orchestration of movement. But all this time our tramp was wandering on in his talk with my aunt. Words like 'death,' 'the war,' 'pheasants,' 'foxes,' stood out and broke through my thoughts about Ted

Lawrence and Mlle. Picquot. They brought me back to the kitchen and the tight pink cheeks and absurdly blue eyes of the man sipping tea from his saucer before me. He was growing sentimental under the gentleness of Aunt Sarah.

'And the end? Well, if it comes to the ditch, I've always been at home in 'em. That'll be going home for good; that's all. I've been a good long way in my time. There's them what are full of fear as to when they're going to die, and where. But what I say is, it's no good your worrying, for you're not going to die until death comes for you. My father died six years ago; yes, six years ago my father died. And it was him as taught me to have no fear.'

At last he got up to go, and we escorted him down the garden path, and helped to load him with his heavy sacks. But even then he could not seem to leave, and kept returning, waving his stick wildly in the air as he talked.

'Well, I'll look you up when I'm passing this way again and just see if you're still alive.' He turned to my old aunt. 'I wonder which of us will die first, you or me?'

He was gone for three years. Aunt Sarah and I looked at each other and smiled.

'That wasn't exactly a wasted morning, was it?' she said.

THE VILLAGE SMITHY

THE SHAPES OF OUR HILLS stand out sharp and distinct as never before, when we are about to quit them for a long journey. Never before had we remarked the beauty of the clump of beech trees above the chalk cross. So it is with the village smithy. Any glimpse of it may be the last. We linger as we pass it, for it might fade before our eyes.

But already the smithy has changed, to meet the needs of the age. Already the few horses that come to be shod are led round by the back way, and the front of the smithy is gay with a row of flaming petrol pumps, like dahlias in full bloom. The clang of hammer on anvil is a rare sound, these days; instead, the cars hoot as they stop to refill by the flaunting dahlias.

But I know a smithy and a blacksmith that do not disappoint. Few horses are to be seen there today, but I have watched a picture as happy as imagination could invent, when Joe Benyon sat on the great white mare and led the chestnut horse by her side, that they might be shod after a day at the plough. I have seen the glow from the smithy forge as I passed at dusk, and smelt the singeing of the white mare's hair.

Everything about this smithy is as it should be. A mighty elm stands close against it, dark blue in the shadows of this August afternoon. There is even a pond in front, reflecting the early winter sunsets and doubling the massive forms of the horses as they wait about its door. Another picture haunts me. A shire horse wades into the pond on a still summer evening, cracking the green duckweed on the surface of the water into circles of brown. On the wooden seat outside the smithy sit three old men talking, and above the murmur of their voices comes the clang of the anvil and hammer.

The blacksmith himself is as traditional as his shop. He is the last sentinel against progress. Talk to him of modern times, and motor-cars and petrol-pumps, and a cloud of anger will pass across his face. He is wise enough to realise his isolation and to know that he is fighting a losing battle; his crusade against speed and noise and rush means more to him than worldly loss or gain. It will be enough, he declares, if he can hold out till death comes for him. He stands at his anvil, fashioning unwanted horseshoes, while less than thirty yards away, at the foot of the lane, roars the traffic on the main road. Its nearness does not concern him, for with hammer and bellows he can drown the endless noise of rushing cars. The smell of the petrol is dimmed by the scent of the hedgerows up the lane, as honeysuckle, wild rose and elder follow each other in the pageant of the year. He has created for himself his own world, and the battlements are strong.

When I think of the blacksmith, my memory turns to a morning in February. I can hear the crackle of wheels crushing the ice of the frozen cart ruts in the lane outside, and the sound of a man jumping heavily to the ground. The half-door of the smithy is closed, for the day is bitter and the wind is a 'lazy wind,' as the blacksmith says, 'a wind that goes through you because it be too lazy to

travel round you.' As I listen to this world of elemental sounds, I can tell by each one of them what is taking place before the smithy. It is Ted's voice that I hear, grunting to his pony as he unfastens the harness and lifts the shafts of the cart high in the air. I can see those shafts standing erect against the grey sky, signal that the smithy is in occupation. And then a shaggy head and shoulders appear, darkly silhouetted above the half-door, muffled against the cold, magenta neckerchief taking on a purple glow as it contrasts with scarlet cheeks. It is Ted Woolcott, the woodman, and he brings with him his pony, Beauty, to be shod. She stands now by his side, her neck springing out with grace against his stocky shoulders, her loosened harness jingling as she shifts the weight of her body from leg to leg.

But Beauty will have to wait. Justin Haynes, the smith, is talking, and there is a pause in the clang of hammer on anvil. Against the heat of the forge stands a strange, wizened creature, stretching out bony hands to the warmth of the embers. As Ted Woolcott unlatches the half-door, he recognises Ebenezer Stopps, the itinerant rat-catcher.

'And how be you these days?' he calls across to him. 'It be many a month since we be a-seeing of you.' But wearily, with no answering smile, Stopps shakes his head.

'Death do be stalking about,' he mutters in a rheumy voice. 'Maybe it be I he be a-looking for. Yes, I do think as how it do be I. I be a old tree blown about by the storm, and I shan't likely see the daffodils again.'

'Come, Ebb,' comforts the blacksmith. 'You ain't got no call to go on like this. It's a bit of warmth as you be a-wanting, and nothing more.'

Beauty whinnies outside, feeling the knives of the wind.

'Why, even that pony of Ted's do dislike the shramming cold,' says Justin Haynes in solace. 'Here, Ted, bring her in and let's see what she do want. All four, do you say?'

And now the elemental sounds follow upon each other in quick succession: the wheezy blowing of bellows, the sharp hammering of the shoe on the anvil as it is held by the long pincers, the sudden sizzle of the pink horseshoe in the well of cold water, the quieter tap of the shoe being nailed to the horse's foot. Cars may tear along the main road, aeroplanes may split the steel-grey of the winter sky, but here in the gloom of the smithy the oldest of crafts lingers, and Justin Haynes hammers and stoops and blows the forge with dignity, as though he were conscious of the antiquity of his trade. But it is not only the weight of his heritage that lends pride to his movements; this working in iron, this heating of iron till it will bend and alter its shape under his mastery, gives to him, each time he fashions a horseshoe, an inevitable feeling of power. It runs through him as the shoe emerges orange from the forge, while the columns of smoke rise from the singed hair of the horse's foot. For he works in the ageless elements of fire and earth.

There is no sunshine this morning to pick out details from the dusty interior. In the darkness of the back of the smithy, behind the forge, lies a muddle of rubbish: old iron, old boxes, disused kitchen stoves, broken garden implements.

Today they are formless gloom, but should the sun come out it would creep past the anvil and light numberless little fires in the derelict metal. It would struggle through the thick dust of the small paned windows, and the clusters of cobwebs would look like wisps of imprisoned smoke. It would turn the brick floor to a gentle red and overrule the glow from the forge. As the morning passed and it grew stronger, it would gild the arms of the blacksmith as he hammered at the anvil and throw a pattern of window panes across the leather of his apron. But the sky is dead grey today and the smithy dark. The presence of Ebb Stopps and Ted Woolcott, gathered round the heat of the forge, is made known to us through our ears as a rumble of talk.

'It be they motor cars what do do me in,' wheezes Ebb Stopps. 'Lor' bless my soul, when I was a young 'un I hadn't never heard tell of they things they call nerves, nor my father, nor his father before him. We did use to go about the country rat-catching all peaceful-like, with nobody making no noise to disturb us. But they motor cars, they rushes upon one so quick, that I reckon I jumps pretty near out of my skin a hundred times a day. And it's that what's doing me in. I tell you, death do be looking around for me, he do.'

The blacksmith pauses in his work, Beauty's hind leg raised and tucked between his knees, as he scrapes her hoof smooth. Bending there by the curving flanks of the pony, the man makes a rhythmic pattern against the sweeping lines of the horse. But he is unaware of it. He only thinks of his enemy the motor car and bursts now into a fury of speech.

'They've driven the horse off the roads, they have, so that a horse these days is pretty near as scarce as hen's teeth. And what do they gain with all their speed, I asks you? They just gets ill, and they aren't happy, and they don't know what to do with the time as they've saved. It all comes to this: the world began to go downhill directly as we got the first motorcar. I can prove it, I can. Now look at me. All I want is to shoe horses in the daytime and to go for a walk up in the woods and the hills in the evening and to dig my allotment. But these days they don't want the earth nohow, they don't. I can prove it, I can. But the earth'll get 'em all in the end. You mark my words.'

Sweat stands upon his face, running down his neck to the striped flannel of his shirt. But it is uncertain whether it is caused by the heat of the forge or hatred of the motor car.

Beauty's fourth shoe is now being fitted and still the rumble of talk goes on in the darkness near the forge. Ted is discussing the villagers, gossiping as he lolls against an old stove. But Ebb does not listen. He presses yet closer to the heat of the embers, quaking with terror as he thinks of the car-infested roads and the shramming cold that awaits him outside. Here, in this warmth, with the great quiet strength of the blacksmith, he feels secure. He has been carried back into the past, to the age to which he belongs.

Justin Haynes has finished shoeing Beauty. He spits on his slate and writes on it what is owing to him from Ted. There is no need now for hurry. There may be no horse today, or tomorrow, or even for a week. Habit, though, runs strong within him, and he blows up the forge, that he may fashion yet more unwanted horseshoes.

As Ted Woolcott leads Beauty out into the knifing cold, he is followed by Ebenezer Stopps.

'I suppose I must be getting along,' wheezes the ratcatcher. 'But somehow or other, it do seem to me that that be my place, in there, along with Justin – and your place, too, by the looks of it. There be some of us what be born too late. And I do reckon that I be one of they.'

THE VILLAGE WITCH

'I shall go into a hare,
With sorrow and sighing and mickle care.
And I shall go in the Devil's name,
Aye, till I come home again.'

BESSIE DOMONEY COMMANDS the village. She lives in the old thatched cottage at the very top of the hill, and nothing can happen in the village without her seeing it. Old, bent, wizened and ugly, she sits motionless at her open door. In summer she will be found outside on her doorstep, but even in winter she merely moves a few feet into the shelter of her cottage; still her door will be open. Witches, it would seem, do not feel the cold. Her familiar, a small black cat called Robin, dozes at her feet, or washes himself, leg lifted upwards in a sinuous curve, when a storm threatens. Bessie watches the life of the village as it passes her doorway. She knows when Mrs. Beveridge goes down the hill to catch the bus to Bridgetown. She notices when Farmer Hutton comes home drunk from the Leather Bottle. The young girls of the village will walk miles across the fields to meet their lovers rather than expose themselves to her stare. For Mrs. Beveridge, Farmer Hutton and the young girls are convinced that old Bessie can see through them and read the thoughts of their minds. Mrs. Beveridge may wrap her purchases tight in brown paper and push them deep into her shopping bag, but unless she should bring back some cigarettes for Bessie, a spell will be cast upon the cheese and bacon she has bought, and her new rayon petticoat will tear in the wash.

It is not only the village people who fear old Bessie. I remember visiting a well-known writer. As he came into his garden to say good bye, the golden sunset tempted him to walk with me across the fields and up the hill to the village. And there he stopped, and turned to leave me. I should have thought nothing of this had I not noticed the frightened look in his face. Intrigued, I tried hard to persuade him to come with me still further. But he refused firmly, and his sensitive face seemed to turn grey at my urgings. I was so puzzled that at last I boldly asked him what was the matter.

'It's like this,' he said. 'You see, I haven't any cigarettes on me just now. And I simply daren't pass Old Bessie if I haven't one to give her. For if you don't give her something as you pass – well, you never know what might happen.'

Poor Old Bessie! She is a pathetic, degenerate relic of the grand old days of witches. It is true that she has her domestic familiar, but not even the most credulous of the villagers has hinted at the existence of her Coven. Her magic is lame and restricted, and doubt is cast upon her allegiance to her master, the Devil. It is whispered, in fact, that she places a bottle

of water in her chimney to keep away evil spirits. And her cat? Does she mix a drop of her own witch's blood with his food when he returns from working magic? I'm afraid not. I fear that the utmost she is supposed to do is to read the Bible to him backwards in the dead of night. Her magic is grown so thin that it is with surprise that one learns that she is even so orthodox as to read it backwards, in the true witch fashion.

And her Sabbaths? Has nobody seen her slip off on her broomstick on All Hallows E'en, or Candlemas, at nine or ten o'clock at night, to join the other witches in their quarterly orgies? I am afraid she does not even possess a besom broom, and the villagers have forgotten the existence of the special Sabbath nights of Lammas or the Eve of May, of Candlemas or the Eve of November. Even if they were to recollect them and should watch out, they would find Old Bessie snoring loudly in her cottage bedroom. For the twentieth-century witch, a sad jumbled product of thinly remembered, time-diluted sayings and fears that have survived only because they are necessary for normal human happiness, is far removed from the benevolent ancient Horn God, and has lost her god-like magical powers. Gone for all time are her 'flying ointments,' of belladonna and aconite, that threw her into a delirious state in which she felt the sensation of flying through the air; gone, too, are her rain-making and fertility rites.

But one thing remains to her, and that is the power of changing herself into a hare. Bessie Domoney is old, these days, and her power fades, but there are grand stories of her magic when she was younger. Matthew Webster will tell you about it, if you ask him seriously and do not laugh at him. It seems that when Matthew had the Rectory Farm, he employed Old Bessie's son as carter. The young man was lazy and one day Matthew lost patience with him and beat him. It was at the edge of the ten-acre field, just by the gate, and Matthew remembers clearly that just as he laid his stick across John Domoney's back, a big hare leapt out of the ditch and crossed his path. Next morning, as he went to his stables to harness Rex and Flossie, he found the two horses worn out and useless. This went on for days, and he could not understand what had happened, until the

cowman told him they must be 'hag-rid.' And sure enough, he met Old
Bessie in the lane and she shouted to him: 'You go and beat my son and so
I go and wear out your horses.' This went on until someone said to him:
'You know what you've got to do. You must hang a wreath of bryony
upside down outside them stables, and that'll break the spell.' And sure
enough, it did, and there were Rex and Flossie as lively again as if nothing
had ever happened.

It is no wonder that Bessie's small, damp cottage is piled high inside
with gifts from the village people. For each of them, be it farmer or literary
gentleman, grave digger or midwife, has much to lose.

But the poor old thing grows old, and her eyes are dim and her mouth
is toothless. Soon she will die, and already her successor has been chosen.
I have never been able to find out how this succession is managed. Did
Susanna Hulbert, Bessie Domoney's predecessor, lay the crown on
Bessie's head, and is it Bessie herself who has chosen Mrs. Drew, from
the white cottage down the church lane, to carry on after her death? I
only know that Mrs. Drew is already spoken of as the next village witch.
Somehow, I feel that she will not be as potently magical as Bessie. I think
that she is wholly benevolent, and I cannot imagine her casting a spell on
anyone. She is a sweet little creature, spending her days in her garden,
among her beehives. She lives for her bees, and her greatest distinction
is the making of mead. But do not suppose that she trades this mead.
On the contrary, it is only to those persons she likes that she will sell it.
And this nectar and ambrosia, this drink of the gods, is stored in prosaic
old beer bottles, with discoloured, age-torn labels dangling from them.
But drink a glass of this magical stuff, eighteen pence a bottle, if you are
chosen by her as being worthy of it, and you will wonder if perhaps she
is not already rehearsing her role as village witch. For surely this feeling
of floating, this sensation of soaring over the hill tops is true witchcraft?
Perhaps she is dispensing some of her magical 'flying ointment.' The
village women will tell you that when they have had a glass of Mrs.
Drew's mead they feel 'all elevated like.' Yes, I think it is quite right that
Mrs Drew should be the next witch.

I have never consciously met another witch, though I have heard many tales of them. I remember a very old man, wizened to look like a pollard willow tree in the winter. He would come to a certain farm in Dorset each morning for water. One day he seemed especially overcast. 'Good morning,' said the farmer's wife. 'And what be the matter with you today? You look vull of trouble and wold.' 'What be the matter with I?' said he. 'God bless my soul, it be they witches at me again. They do come and sow nettles and weed seeds all over my garden. They do blow smoke through my keyhole at night so as I can't sleep for the hurt to my eyes. They do walk about and steal my things.'

The farmer's wife told me that this happens to him every few weeks, and that then he informs the postman, who sends the local police sergeant along to him to put things right. His witches seem poor things, who have lost their supernatural power; else how should they be forced to subject themselves to the English law? It makes one very sad.

And then, also in Dorset, there was Old Galpin, the wheelwright, who confided to me that his mother had destroyed a witch. 'That hare would come in each day and do harm, until my mother put a broomstick athwart the door. The very next morning the witch came in person and says: 'You've broken me, Mrs. Galpin. I can't do no more to you now.'

I had expected and hoped to find witches in the Chiltern Hills. I believe that they do still exist, but it is hard to get the villagers to admit to them. Generally, the very old people have grown muddled and incoherent, taking with themselves to the grave their tangled memories of witchcraft. One old man, who should have known, hastened to assure me that there were none these days. 'Why,' he said, 'you could go right through all they beech woods at midnight and never meet no one.' And he seemed proud that it should be so, and yet more proud that he should be up-to-date enough to ridicule the idea of them. He did not know how deeply he disappointed me. For our beech woods are made for witches, those creatures that escaped to the fastnesses of the hills. In the dips of these hills, behind the prehistoric chalk cross – relic in itself of the days of their supremacy – are small sheltered clearings, screened from the world by the surrounding beech woods. Here, surely, among the juniper bushes, is the place for the witches' Sabbath. I do not believe that my old man was telling me the truth. Perhaps he was even trying to mislead me. Perhaps, in fact, he is himself a witch.

At any rate, I am still searching.

PICKING PRIMROSES

IT ALL CAME OVER ME ONE MORNING as I smelt a bud of the flowering currant. A pleasing trickle of fear ran through my body. So insistent was it that I stopped still, asking myself its cause. Here was I, walking safely round my own garden on a spring morning, and yet trembling with terror. I looked about me, but everything was just as usual – the grass paths, the trees, the daffodils. And then I understood. I was back at the edge of a wood, as a small child, and in the ditch grew a bush of flowering currant, strayed oddly from its fellows in the gamekeeper's cottage nearby. This stinging, acrid smell had ripped the years aside, and I had gone primrosing.

But why, you may ask, this terror? Why this trembling fear? What has it to do with picking primroses? Could anything be more idyllic, more blissful?

Looking back on it all now with the values of an adult, I admit that it is hard to understand the intensity of the terror we children felt. But isn't this always so? Would even the horrors of war be worse to us than were the horrors of darkness when we were small? The crunch of feet on the gravelled path at midnight has power now to distress me as I remember the anguish of my childhood at the dustman's nocturnal visits. I might know that it was only the dustman, but that did nothing to lessen the shaking, sweating terror I felt as, awakened suddenly from deep sleep by the creak of the heavy cart, I listened to it moving nearer and nearer to our house. How clearly now I hear the feet of the dustman as he climbed the front steps and crunched his way round to the dustbin at the back; how accurately I note the rise and fall in that pattern of sound. And as I hid my head under the bedclothes, that I might not see the lantern light dancing across the ceiling, or hear the jangled tossing of the horse's harness, I believe I touched then the depth of human fear. What was it that gave me this fear? Was it merely the sudden light, the abrupt waking out of deep sleep? Perhaps it was the formlessness of it all that lent strength to my imaginings; for I never once dared to get out of bed and look at the dustman or his cart. At any rate, I find that in retrospect I associated the heavy dust cart in my mind with the tumbrils of the French Revolution. Again, in memory's ears I hear that dustman's voice calling: 'Bring out your dead! Bring out your dead!' But I find myself wondering at what age these associations crept into my mind, for I am by no means sure that at that age I had heard either of the French Revolution or the Plague.

But I was talking about picking primroses, and I was going to tell you why I remember it with such pleasant fear.

Our family had a house on the East Coast, and no sooner had we migrated there at Easter time than this annual urge would come upon us children. It may be that if our house had been in Sussex or Kent or Devon this would never have happened; for there, where the lanes and banks are studded with spring flowers, like the paintings of the Early Italians, the primrose is not the rare thing that it was to us in our bleak countryside.

As it was, the only primroses that grew anywhere near were in two particular woods. And these two woods were private property. What is more, they were fenced and wired and watched, for they contained pheasants.

'Now then, Miss Clare and Master Evelyn, what about going primrosing today?' Old Nurse would suggest. 'It'll be Miss Clare's birthday come round before you know where you are, m'say, and what'll you feel like with no primroses for the birthday tea?'

In the rituals of our childhood's year, my iced birthday cake needed to be surrounded by stolen primroses. No mere flora, they had been gathered with the ecstasy of great fear. There was something almost sacrificial about them, an offering to the god of courage and adventure. Had they been picked in the garden, they would have held no magic.

How well I remember those walks along the Yarmouth road, with my brothers and the old nurse. It was queer how this strict Baptist, normally so straitlaced and upright, would fling aside her moral scruples and organise this reckless trespassing. She strode the country road, a predatory light in her eyes impatient of the slow pace of our small legs. Larks sang in the blue sky, and gorse shone golden around us, and clumps of daisies sprang from the soft turf beneath our feet. But all the while that we walked this road our minds were filled with the central fear: *should we be caught?*

'Now then, Master Roland, no hanging about like that. You're very near enough to drive one crazy.'

Like sheep to the slaughter, we were driven on by the old woman. But,

oh, it was a sweet, delicious slaughter, amid sulphur-coloured woods and moss and birds in the hazel trees.

At last, with all our dallying, we reached the slight twist in the road that disclosed the gamekeeper's cottage at the foot of the slope. And now our tension increased. Our hands tightened round the handles of our empty baskets till it pained us. We slithered to the far side of our nurse, ungallantly exposing her to the possible eyes of the gamekeeper or his wife. We hid those empty baskets as best we could in the ample folds of her thick grey skirts; but it was with little conviction that we did so, for we were certain of the magical powers of the gamekeeper's wife, that would enable her not only to see through matter, but to divine the thoughts in our minds as we crept past her cottage.

But whereas, until we reached the cottage we were continuously searching for pretexts to go back home, once we were past it, it was safer to go on, and with a comparatively light heart we swung by the yellow powdery pussy willow tree and rushed in at the lane to the woods.

It was to this lane that the flowering currant had strayed. True to ritual, we children picked a clump of blossom, pinching it to make the smell stronger and more stinging. It resembled somewhat the stoop of holy water at the entrance to a church, so full of awe were we. And it was here and now that our ways parted. To the left of the lane lay the friendly wood, to the right the dark, dense, terrifying wood into which only my elder brother ventured. Throughout the many years of this annual primrosing, I got no further than a timid creep into the fringe, though I knew that in its black depths bloomed primrose and wood sorrel, violets and wood anemones such as were to be found nowhere else. But in its depths, too, lurked all the evil spirits of creation, and in the very centre of that blackness lived the Devil himself. I never ceased to wonder when my brother emerged unchanged and safe. I remember now the exact whirr of the frightened pheasants that he raised as he snapped the undergrowth; I can see the clumsy rush of a disturbed wood pigeon. But as I crouched beside a clump of primroses in the wood on the left, I imagined each of these creatures to be, not normal bird, but my brother bewitched by that Devil in the dark wood.

Does every child mark down some dwelling place for the Devil? Mine followed me about, and whereas he lived in this wood in the summer half of the year, during the winter, when the family were in London he, too, moved, and took up his residence in the ventilator, shaped like a giant's top hat, in the middle of the lake in Regent's Park. Never did my old nurse guess of the agonies I endured as we passed this part of the lake on our daily walks.

And this sets one wondering whether it may not be normal and desirable to have some fear in one's life. Civilisation has deprived us of so many of the primitive causes of fear, but has it at the same time rid us of the need for them? Are we not perhaps living with one side of our nature unsatisfied? Might not the physiologist have something to say about this? And is it for this reason that we gratuitously seek out fear? I am remembering my bewilderment in visiting an alligator farm in Florida. Six thousand alligators lived and bred there. But why? I asked. Their skins were not used for purses. And then I realised what it all meant. They supplied a felt want. They supplied a safe thrill of fear. There, where life was soft and easy, the Florida holidaymaker needed the stimulation of terror. So the wise coloured man beguiled us into the breeding pen, where the grey reptiles lay shamming sleep, ready at any moment to whack at us with their cased tails. 'You sho better take care, mam,' crooned the negro attendant. 'That ole' fellar over there, he snap you if you don't move quick, right along now. Yes, mam.' And one got an authentic prehistoric fright, trickling all the way down one's back, and stimulating one's adrenals. It felt good.

What does it matter if one of us gets this thrill through alligators, and another through picking primroses? The great thing is to get it, and if possible to be able to call it up at will. Each time I see a flower woman standing with her basket of primroses on the kerb of a London street, or meet a straggling clump of village children with their hands full of tightly-clenched bunches, I can cast my mind back across the years and re-live that extravaganza of emotion.

Yes, I am once more in the wood on the left of the lane, where the sun shines upon the crowded primroses through the bare branches of the hazel trees. I am so busy picking that I notice nothing, neither time nor bird nor sound. I have strayed far from my nurse, and as I pause to tie a piece of white wool round a bunch, I look for her; but she is hidden from me. I grow frightened, and would run. And then I hear a crackling sound as the lower branches of the hazel trees are brushed aside. I look up, thinking it to be my nurse. But there stands before me and above me a mighty man. His knees are on a level with my face, his head is misty among the topmost branches of the hazel trees. It is the owner of the woods. I cannot hide. I cannot run. I crouch where I am, and wait. And as I wait, an extraordinary thing happens. This mighty man does not speak, or hit me or order me from his woods. He smiles, and passes on. I wait and my nurse finds me; but my basket is only half filled, and I cry to be taken home.

And then? Yes, I remember what happened then. We went to those same woods, primrosing, a day or two later. But the entrance to the woods, down the little lane, was blocked with barbed wire, and we returned home with empty baskets.

The owner had forgotten his smile.

THE VILLAGE FAIR

THE ELEPHANT LUMBERED down the village street. His feet crushed the buttercups that grew at its edge, sprinkling a film of gold dust upon the coarse hide of his legs. The breeze tossed the flowering chestnuts by the farm gates, shaking down stray blossoms that alighted on the elephant's back as he passed: so had the blossoms of the mango tree stroked his hide in India as they fell. For shade of jungle he had now the gloom under the chestnut trees, for glare of tropical sun but the kindly warmth of an English May.

The camel shuffled pompously along the village street. As he walked, his feet struck against the dust of the dry country road; but it was hard and resisting to the touch as compared with the sand of his African desert. A pony and cart passed him with a neat little patter of hooves; the camel dilated his nostrils further, till he looked like a disdainful Chinese terracotta of the T'ang period.

But the sounds both of elephant tread and camel shuffle were lost beneath the rumble of many tarpaulin-covered lorries, and the clang of the conducting traction engine, its twisted brass decorations catching the sun and vibrating as it moved. Smoke curled from its funnel, waved by the breeze until it tied traction engine to lorry, and dipped to encircle the camel's neck.

The village dozed in the warmth of the May afternoon. Street and window and cottage garden were alike empty. Even the village shop, with its blind lowered against the sun, looked asleep. But as the tarpaulin-covered lorries and the traction engine rattled through the street, cottage windows shook; in the empty bar of the Wheatsheaf the glasses on the shelves clinked against each other as they quivered. The rumble of the fair subdued even the sound of the smithy bellows.

Heads appeared at windows. The landlord of the Wheatsheaf wakened from his nap. The shrill whistle of the traction engine wove itself into Mrs. Durling's dream, till she got up with a start, imagining herself running along the platform to catch a train that was already moving.

People came to their cottage doors. Miss Stacey's eyes pierced the tarpaulins, discovering the glories that were hidden beneath. She did not seem to notice the elephant or the camel. Her eyes divined, blazoned against the dusty coverings, a bright turquoise blue vase, gold fluted, ornamented with a picture of a lovely lady holding a rose. It was what her mantelpiece needed, alongside the scarlet vase with the Japanese lady on it that she had won at the Bang All fair last autumn. In the crowds and the shadows of the evening no one would recognise her at the darts. For days now she had gazed with longing at the notice, heralding the fair, that had been pasted on the trunk of the sycamore tree by the bus halt.

Amy Simmonds was kitchen maid at the rectory. The crockery in the pantry shook, and she knew that this trembling meant the arrival of the fair. Background of sink and dishcloth faded and before her she saw a golden dragon and a painted pony; and on one of them she was sitting and on the other Henry. The air was full of yellow music as she and Henry rode on and away. Henry was leaning over to her on her golden dragon and he was – but she grew ashamed of her thoughts, and blushed. Cook called to her from the kitchen, but she did not hear. She rushed from the pantry to the back gate, in time to watch the last of the covered lorries pass. Through the tarpaulin the eye of faith could behold her golden dragon and Henry's painted pony.

But in the village school the children could see nothing. The windows were high, and all that was visible before their eyes was a large map of India unrolled upon the distempered wall. Suddenly the whole of India shook, and the wild flowers in jam jars on the teacher's table trembled. A loud rumble outside grew nearer and yet louder. Twenty-three small bodies tautened and simultaneously twenty-three minds wandered. Miss Moody rapped upon her desk with a pencil, but the geography lesson had lost its grip and India had retreated to its normal place beyond the horizon.

Twenty-three pairs of eyes watched the procession of the fair through the village street, matching heard sounds to imagined visions, unobstructed by map, distempered wall, masonry and brick. Miss Moody's voice went on unheeded, as she spoke of the animals that lived in India.

'There are monkeys and snakes and tigers and lions and elephants'

'Elephants!' The word jerked itself into Betty Cole's dreamings. 'Elephants! Why, that notice said there'd be an elephant at the fair, same as there was last time. Yes, a real elephant to ride on!'

Across the unrolled map of India lumbered an elephant.

'Five and two's seven and nine's one-and-four. And with the sixpence Uncle Charlie's promised me that'll make one-and-ten. Enough for the coco-nuts and twice on the roundabout.'

'Johnny! You're not listening. Now what animals did I say there are in India?'

'Golden dragons and painted ponies and spotted giraffes and huge bright cocks,' answered Johnny promptly, with unexpected excitement.

On the village green, just past the church, there was commotion. The traction engine had conducted its family of lorries and stood now apart, silent and smokeless. With unbelievable speed booths had been erected, till the place was like a fugue in stripes: wide, narrow, vertical, horizontal, yellow, red, blue, white. And as stripe repeated stripe, to be matched by a background of half-timbering, so did the shape of peaked stall repeat that of peaked gable, rising to its crescendo in the speared peak of church steeple behind, till a rhythm ran through the whole, and village and fair made one pattern.

It was not only the booths that had appeared with such speed. With the rapidity of the nomad the travellers had established themselves. Caravans of yellow ochre and Indian red had resumed their interrupted family life; stoves and cooking utensils had been dumped upon the floor by their side, to be guarded by cur-like dogs that were chained to the wheels. The spaces beneath the caravans had been turned into hen runs, and anxiously clucking fowls investigated their latest netting-bound homes. Inside the vans a few of the travellers slept on their bunks, tousled heads and stockinged feet visible from the open doors at the back. Others were busy behind awnings, dusting the treasures they would display that night. Coco nuts were balanced on the top of painted posts, roundabouts were fixed, and shabby electric lights drooped beneath their dirty tasselled shades. From an especially imposing caravan on the outskirts came the ugly shrieks of old Ma Polligrew, demanding paraffin for her cooking stove. Hideous and deaf, she yet was the boss of the show, and burly men rushed to obey her.

But the first feeling of excitement in the village had faded. As the sultry afternoon moved on, and Jim Bentwich arranged the prizes on 'Mother's Day Out,' he grew low-spirited.

'A one-eyed hole this is, and no mistake,' he muttered. 'Hardly worth the trouble of stopping here, it isn't. Now what I like is a place where everyone sort of seems to get all excited. When I recollect the days when I was a young'un, when there weren't no buses, and folks didn't rush into Wycombe or Aylesbury to see the pictures and get to know all about all sorts of things that aren't no good to them – why, this place seems full of nothing but earwigs like that dried-up old girl poking about round Abe's show. Wonder what she can want.'

He little guessed at the excitement in the breast of Miss Stacey as she peeped inside the awnings in search of her turquoise-blue vase.

Into the silence now of the village trickled the sound of a rusty gramophone, reposing in a child's broken-down mail-cart. Like spindrift washed up by the waves, the old cripple had arrived on the high tide of the fair, and pushed his discordant music before him, hoping to profit by heightened emotions. But the street was nearly empty. Only Miss Stacey dropped a penny into his greasy, upturned cap as she passed: a libation to the gods, in whose hands rested her turquoise-blue vase.

But it was something more subtle than the heat of the afternoon that kept the villagers indoors. They were feeling unconscious resentment at this sudden invasion of their privacy. It was one thing to enjoy yourself at the fair after dark, with everybody making a noise and no one to be certain whether you were there or not, but it was quite another thing to have to come face to face with these brazen hussies and evil-looking dark men in broad daylight in your own village street. They might at least have the decency to keep inside their caravans until dusk, the bouncing creatures. But lush and bountiful they were, with an alien beauty, as they strode the village with their deep-chested figures and their rich lips.

'There's a wicked look about them,' thought Miss Heathorn, the village dressmaker, as she pushed aside her ferns and peeped through her heavily-curtained window. 'And there they go marching along so happy-like, just as though they were the only ones what knew how to live. What beats

me is those lovely children of theirs – just like little angels, and looking as though they would put on wings any moment and dance.'

School had ended and the fair ground now was loud with shouting and agitated with pointing arms and running figures. The elephant and the camel were surrounded. Each side show was eagerly examined. And as the children's excitement grew, it infused the fair with life, till the dirty electric light hangings ceased to look dowdy and the gilt decorations lost their tawdriness. Their shrieks instilled magic into the cluster of covered shacks and garish vans, and turned the unwashed showmen into figures of wizardry. It did not matter that the awnings had not yet been removed from the booths, or that the Wild West Cowboys walked about in ordinary attire; these deficiencies merely added to the feeling of glamour. As each new sign was erected, each mystery disclosed, there was a gasp of breath. The children were spectators at the creation of a new world.

The Reverend Maurice Norton was going home to his tea. With eyes lowered to the ground, he avoided seeing anything of the fair about him. Perhaps there wasn't really anything wrong in a fair, but you never quite knew, and it was better to be on the safe side. Just as he was leaving the fair ground to branch off to his house, he lifted his eyes. There, before him, was a closed tent and on it, in enormous letters, was written WONDERS NEVER CEASE. CLEAN, CLEVER, and ARTISTIC. By the side of the tent stood a young woman of amazing beauty such as the Reverend Maurice Norton had never before beheld. Hastily he looked away, but before his lowered eyes he still saw those words: WONDERS NEVER CEASE. CLEAN, CLEVER, and ARTISTIC. The longer he walked the more they burnt into his brain, till he paused at his garden gate, fearing lest Mrs. Norton should also see them flaming before his eyes. He went for a walk, to calm himself. But unwittingly his feet turned towards the fair, and soon he found himself staring once more at the closed tent. Should he visit it that evening? After all, the notice said it was CLEAN. What was it inside there that was CLEAN? Why not go and see? Should he? Should he not?

In the gathering heat of the May evening the fair waited.

At six o'clock exactly it began, smashing the quiet of the village. Each separate sound, the roar and the music of the roundabouts, the shouts of the showmen, the drums of the Wild West Cowboys, rose simultaneously like the song of the birds' choir at dawn. And stirred in their houses by this sudden rush of noise, the villagers put aside their calm and hurried outdoors. The fair-ground swarmed with people, as though it were a disturbed ant-heap.

In the windless heat of the village green, midges floated around in mists, settling on the light frocks of the girls, slipping into people's eyes, tickling their faces.

'It be going to be a storm,' thought old George Gregory, as he hobbled along to the Saracen's Head for his evening chat. 'And yet the sky do look that clear. But it don't do to go by the sky. It's they midges what do tell the tale.'

Dusk fell, dimming the background line of hills; the jagged clutter of the fair ground gave them by contrast a look of enduring calm, even as they in their turn emphasised the fleeting dazzle of the fair. The pale green of the sky changed to steel-blue, and as the rival light faded from the heavens, so the lights of the fair grew more imposing and various. The people's faces blushed or blanched, according as they visited a booth with pink, or yellow or pale white-blue illumination; they looked as though suffused by sudden emotion. The lights threw their shafts upwards upon the young leaves of the chestnuts, turning them to soft yellowy-green against a Prussian-blue sky. They played odd pranks now with the shapes of side-shows and booths, casting long shadows in all directions, till it was hard to tell where one booth ended and the next began. They picked out the transparent awnings with a rich glow, leaving the opaque ones in darkness. The roundabouts floated on circles of inky black.

And into this chaos of lights was woven a jumble of smell and sound. Fish and chips mingled with the sticky smell of burnt sugar and overpowered the scent of the trodden grass. Before the Wild West Show the cowboys beat their drums and blared their attractions through loudspeakers, playing on their electric organ: 'Is it true what they say about Dixie?' that it might charm the villagers into the atmosphere of the American prairie. So loud were the noises from this Show, that they almost drowned the shout of the man with the horses at The Spinning Jenny, and made the bursting of air balloons into nothing of more moment than the popping of a broom pod on a hot day.

The noise silenced the arrival of the Wycombe and Aylesbury buses. The newcomers blinked at the sudden blaze of light, bewildered to find

themselves caught up into this rushing current of movement and sound. And as they were drawn into the centre of this human whirlpool, the music of the roundabouts melted their restraints and played tricks with time, so that the old ones among them unfolded the past and surrendered themselves. Their bodies drifted about the fair in a dazed state, but their minds were bewitched.

Mrs. Leamy had come in by bus to visit her granddaughter. As she crossed the fair ground, winding her way with difficulty through the thick patterning of the crowd, she, too, flung back her years. 'I mind me of the day when Luke took me to Aylesbury Fair,' she murmured to herself, as was her habit. 'We hadn't been walking out but since April. "Gal," he says, I must buy you a fairing. What'll you have? "Now, lad," I says to him, "don't you be getting me no fairings." But he would do it. Yes, Luke, you would do it. "Well," I says, "then you get me a dolly and that'll do for our little 'uns when they come." And Luke and I, we blushed that red. Didn't we, now, Luke? Fairs was a different thing in they days. Come to think of it, I mind me of the hiring fair, and Luke standing there wearing a bit o' sheep's wool and looking that strong and proud and me trying to look as if he didn't belong to me no how. And then Farmer Bletcher comes along and gives him the shilling, and Luke puts a bit of ribbon in his hair to show as he was hired, and off we goes to enjoy ourselves. Ah, they was fairs in they days. Not like this sort of a thing.'

Mrs. Leamy's murmurings grew fainter as she left the fair ground for her granddaughter's cottage.

But Amy Simmonds did not need to play any tricks with time. Her world was here, and now, and she was this evening weaving the fabric of which her memories would consist when she should have reached Mrs. Leamy's age. So, perhaps, in fifty years from tonight, she, too, would look back upon this fair, and murmur how times had changed. For Amy was with her Henry.

She floated through the crowds upon his arm, remote from her surroundings, even while she was herself a vital unit in the jumbled pattern. Her body was disturbed by such thrills that she did not notice that the boys had started to tumble the girls. Bags of confetti were bought, to be thrust down the girls' chests. The thin surface of civilisation was being peeled off, and primitive man struggled with his woman on the ground; it made no difference that it was Jim Shelby, the grocer's lad, who was searching down Connie Mason's frock, that he might recover the confetti he had poked between her breasts. From the shadows behind booths came shrieks and giggles, and sounds of struggle. Escaping girls leapt across patches of light, loitering that they might again be caught. But though Amy's blood ran as high as any, she had the reticence of the romantic.

It was some time before they reached the roundabout, and it was then that Amy started to cry. For there was no golden dragon. They were all ponies. She had set her heart on her golden dragon and the magic faded from life. The ponies became mere blocks of carved wood, gaudily painted. With difficulty Henry made her notice the difference between each pony, pointing out their golden manes, their crimson nostrils. 'And look!' he said. 'They've each of them got a name. Let's see if there's an Amy or a Henry! Look! Doris and Robert, Sidney and Mabel, Alfred and Dolly and – yes, look! Henry and Amy!' Strange though it may seem, it was the truth. And they mounted the ponies and rode away, till the confining circle of the roundabout broke and shot to the skies.

Meanwhile Miss Stacey was feeling hot and worried. She could not find her turquoise-blue vase. There, on one of the stalls, were green china rabbits with black glass eyes, black dogs, fern pots decorated with pictures of deserts and palm trees and camels; in one corner, even, a crimson china swan with red-gold wings. She visited another stall, to find it covered with glass butter dishes she didn't want and bright-coloured balls and fur dogs. She had turned in disappointment from a third stall, when she noticed a dazzle of white at the far end. She went closer, and saw that it was a white plaster statuette of some naked lady – Venus, she was called.

Miss Stacey stared at her. And as she stared, a great longing filled her for the beauty of this female figure. Emily Stacey thought of her own withered, deformed body, with its twisted hip and its wrinkled skin. She thought of all she had missed in life, and of her unreturned love for Harry Southwell, years back. This, then, was what a woman should look like. Those were the curves that lay hidden from sight under the cotton frocks of the village girls. That was the way your hips should balance and swing. Nervously Miss Stacey felt down her own side, touching the bones of her body with distaste. She must have that statuette to look at always. No matter what the village thought, she yet must have it. She hesitated for one moment as she wondered what the rector would say. But wasn't there something about someone called Venus a long, long while ago? That, surely, would make it all right. It wasn't as though it were the figure of someone nowadays.

Her mind set, Miss Stacey threw a dart. There was nobody she knew near the stall at that minute. It was her chance. She threw another, and yet another, till she had earned her Venus. But at this point her luck turned.

'Good evening, Miss Stacey,' said a shrill voice at her side. 'Having a try for something? What'll you be choosing? One of them blue willow-pattern teapots is what I'd have in your place. Coo! Look at that naked lady! Now whoever'd want that!'

Miss Stacey trembled as she recognised the voice of Mrs. Brown, the baker's mother-in-law.

'Yes,' she said faintly, 'I was thinking of choosing the teapot, too.'

Four times this night did Miss Stacey win a prize at the darts, and four times the same thing happened, until she found herself burdened with unwanted teapot and butter dish, glass bowl and cup and saucer. But she did not give up hope, and as the church clock struck ten she still awaited her moment.

It was the Wild West Show that drew the greatest crowd. Between each performance, the cowboys and their show girl strode the open stage at the front of their booth, twisting their lassos into snaky coils, beating their drums, exhibiting their leather steel-studded trousers, their wide hats. And the touch of the exotic thrilled the villagers, till it needed but the sense of

possible danger to send their blood leaping and pounding through their bodies. For there, too, on the stage before them, stood the American sharpshooter, the idol of the male youth of the neighbourhood. 'Ladies especially welcomed,' shouts the sharpshooter as he lets off a few sampling shots. But it is a company of males that prepares to rush into the booth for the next performance.

'See the lady defying death at each second!' declares the notice across the top of the booth. 'See a missionary in the hands of the Sioux Indians!' proclaims a twisting scrawl up the side of the opening.

But if the Wild West Show excited the villagers, it did yet more for Ernie Tucker. Short and thin, he slipped in for each performance without paying, diving under the arm of the man before him. And there, throughout the evening, he stood at the very front of the show, smoking a stolen clay pipe. Something had happened this evening. Rebellion had entered into him. Never again would he obey his father and run errands for him after school hours, carrying his heavy baskets of fruit and vegetables. He knew suddenly what he was. He was a man among men. And with this realisation he saw his father as a feeble, tired little village fruiterer, and he stood with his legs apart and removed his clay pipe from his mouth and spat.

But the show was due to begin. The table was laden with knives and tomahawks, swords and pistols. And in a pile at one end were the clay pipes, ready to be shot away. On the walls of the tent were brightly-coloured advertisements of Winchester rifles, taking the eye and the mind to foreign parts. That view of the Rocky Mountains forced you far from England and a village green. But Ernie Tucker did not need this dope.

The constricting walls of the tent had disappeared and the trodden grass beneath his feet had changed already into the buffalo pastures of the great Wild West prairies. He brandished a large open penknife and threw it at the woodwork of the raised platform, killing many Indians as he did so.

'Coo! If that ain't Ernie Tucker over there, pretending to smoke a pipe! 'E won't arf catch it when 'is dad finds out where 'e is,' said a voice close behind him. But Ernie Tucker was too far away to hear.

While Ernie was attaining an abrupt maturity, other children had been put to bed. A wind had risen and it wafted the music of the fair across fields and lanes to the cottages of neighbouring villages. And as the sound came into their bedrooms, children slipped from the sheets and tiptoed to the windows, to look across the black fields at the fair, sparkling golden against the night sky.

'Wonder what that elephant looks like at night,' thought one. 'And that camel,' thought another. 'And the painted ponies and those Wild West cowboys,' thought a third.

But it was not only the children who heard the music. Mrs. Bradshaw got up and put on her stockings as an especially loud passage of the music floated in through her bedroom window. There is nothing so sad to the human heart as the realisation of the death of a rapture, and Mrs. Bradshaw wept.

'To think that when I was young I'd have walked five miles to go to a fair, and now, when it's just outside my door, as you might say, I goes to bed.'

She stumbled across her room and picked up her stays. But they struck cold against her body, and she found herself putting them back on to the chair and crossing again to the bed.

'You're nothing but a stupid old woman,' she told herself. 'What be you a-doing of, thinking you are going out gadding at this time of night?'

The wind was kind and swerved to the east, so that the music from the fair became muted and ceased to worry her. Quietly she sighed, and, sighing, fell asleep.

But the wind was less kind to the Reverend Maurice Norton. As it swerved, it brought to his house the full strength of the music of the fair.

The poor man had spent the evening in a torment.

'Looks as if we're going to have a storm,' he kept on saying to Mrs. Norton. 'I think I'll just pop outside and have a look round.'

Several times he went into the garden and opened the gate and walked towards the fair. Before his eyes in the night sky he saw in flaming letters WONDERS NEVER CEASE. CLEAN, CLEVER, and ARTISTIC. In his senses he beheld a young woman of extreme beauty. So brightly did the words stand before him that they hurt his eyes, as though he were gazing at molten steel. He rushed indoors and opened a newspaper.

As Mr. Norton undressed to go to bed, he enjoyed none of the emotions of the victor. Instead, he grew philosophical.

'There's nothing that can put back time,' he told his pyjamas. 'Now I shall never know what was inside that tent. And guessing isn't much of a help.'

It was just as he lay in bed, beside Mrs. Norton, that the wind swerved and brought to him in full force the music of the fair.

'They oughtn't to be allowed to make all that noise so late at night,' grumbled Mrs. Norton as she turned round to sleep. 'Upsetting one like this!'

Mr. Norton writhed in anguish. 'Yes, it does upset one, doesn't it?' he answered. And before his eyes in the darkness flamed the words of temptation.

Up at the manor house Cecilia Stanton heard the music of the fair. Like the Reverend Maurice Norton, she was troubled. She, too, was drawn by it and resisted. But for her the attraction was no lush beauty standing by the opening of a booth. Her maid that afternoon had told her of the soothsayer who was coming with the fair.

'And I shall visit her, mam, just to see what she says about me and my Bert. There'll not be many of us girls as won't go in and see what she's got to tell us. They say she's wonderful, and a real Egyptian.'

But Cecilia had not yet made up her mind. Standing at the library window, she saw the golden glare across the fields, and thought of the crowds she would have to face and the eyes that would look at her in astonishment. The only thing to do was to wrap herself thickly in scarves and cloak, that she might not be recognised.

Cecilia Stanton was childless. Through the early years of her marriage it had been a matter of no importance to her, but now, as she grew older, it hurt continuously. She found herself turning from the sight of a cat with her kittens, or a mother bird on her nest, with a sick ache inside her.

'And now,' she thought, 'now perhaps I shall know. They say she's a real gypsy. If only she will give me some hope. And I need never tell a soul that I've been.'

With these words she knew she had decided.

There was an air of great mystery about the soothsayer's tent, with its carefully drawn, dirty, yellow curtains. 'Patronised by Royalty in 1926 and 1927,' boasted a notice across the front, above a smeared photograph of the gypsy family. The soothsayer stood invitingly outside her tent, waiting. In the heat of this May evening, she looked a strange figure in her bedraggled fur coat, a billow of bright scarves foaming at her neck and chest, and escaping down the front of her black velvet skirt. Cecilia Stanton followed her into the tent with reluctance, wondering now why she had come. But it was too late to draw back, for the mysterious yellow curtains had been pulled tightly across the opening. They were alone together.

Regardless of the electric light that hung from the ceiling of the tent, the gypsy lit a little oil lamp. The match, as she struck it, exposed her filthy hands with their black nails and mass of heavy rings. With those hands she caught hold of one of Cecilia's, with its manicured finger-nails.

'Did she ever wash?' wondered Cecilia, nearly choking with the imprisoned heat and the smell of the soothsayer's body. On the wall behind her hung a flag, its scarlet lion rampant seeming as though at any moment it would clutch at the greasy hair of the gypsy as she bent over her hand.

The soothsayer trickled on, telling of everything except the one subject that mattered. Cecilia let her mind wander and studied the pattern of the green tasselled tablecloth, and the hangings of dirty white lace curtains. On the wall opposite were pictures of hands and heads. A pack of dirty playing cards and a chipped crystal lay on the table by her side.

'And children?' asked Cecilia, trying to sound casual. 'Don't you see any children?'

But the soothsayer shook her head.

'They're dim,' she said, 'very dim.'

Cecilia Stanton moved into the dazzle of the fair. As she turned away she recognised a young girl standing by the next booth. It was Lucy, the kitchen maid she had lately dismissed. And Lucy was heavy with child.

The fair went on. The stars in the sky had disappeared unnoticed. Without that magic circle of light the countryside grew darker and darker. Not a leaf shook on the trees. The air was hot and still and lay heavy upon the earth. Within the circle of the fair, though they did not perceive it, the people were charged with this same feeling of expectancy. The force that came down from the sky was the same that frightened the birds in the bushes, though it altered its effect as it struck each person. Miss Stacey only knew that her desire for her Venus was growing unbearable; Henry and Amy thought that love had never before in this world meant so much. The giggles of the girls grew stronger, the boys became yet more bold. Above the roar and rattle of the fair, the elephant lifted up his trunk and bellowed. Unconsciously everyone waited.

It was then that it happened. Brighter even than the illumination of the fair, pierced the sudden lightning. Louder than the elephant's bellow came the roar of the thunder. Quicker than the rush of the roundabout swept the night wind. It lifted the coverings of the stalls; it tossed the wooden supports as if they had been match sticks. Terror entered into the heart of the elephant: he ran amuck, and as he plunged through the fair, the crowds divided before him, like the parting of the sea before the bows of a ship. Shrieks were covered up by thunder; white faces seemed yet whiter in the sudden flashing of the lightning. The rain came down upon the chaos like stinging whips, but it did not loosen the tension.

On the Wild West prairies, a pale, mean-looking little boy was shooting Indians. Bang went the pistol of the American sharpshooter; outside in the heavens roared the thunder; the lightning became the flashes of a shot. It was only when the electric current failed, and darkness fell upon the tightly-packed crowd in the Wild West Show that Ernie Tucker noticed the storm.

But Miss Stacey had had her moment. Just before the lights went out, she had seized it. In the confusion of the storm she could throw her darts unwatched. Rapidly she caught up her white statuette and ran. As she went, burdened with unwanted butter dish and teapot, glass bowl and cup and saucer, she clutched tight hold of the naked Venus. But somebody hit against her in the darkness and she slipped. The raindrops mingled with her tears as Miss Stacey crept home to bed.

But perhaps it was the landlord of the Wheatsheaf who was feeling as disgruntled as anybody. He sat at the window of his closed bar and swore.

'If there had to be a storm, why on earth did it have to wait until ten minutes past closing time?' he grumbled. 'To think of all the folks I could have had in here, if it'd been but one hour earlier. It's what I call the worst luck a fellow could have had.'

The sun shone next morning with the freshness of a May day after a storm. Early as the villagers had risen, the fair had been still earlier. It had disappeared. And so completely had it disappeared, and with so little noise, that several people who were more fanciful than the rest were inclined to wonder if it had existed at all outside their own imagination. It was a tempting thought, that might have developed one day into a legend.

But one thing remained. There, in the very middle of the village street, lay a heap of crushed white plaster. As Miss Stacey went across the street in the morning light, she paused and looked at the broken pieces. But it was no good. Her Venus was lost for ever.

CHAIR BODGERS

IT WAS A MORNING IN MAY. Never had the beech woods looked more magical. The sunshine played with them. It splashed the tree trunks with dappled light, till they danced and sparkled and forgot that they were solid columns of wood. It touched the leaves and transformed them. It turned them to silver when they faced the sun; it dyed them yellow when they backed it; it left them green and ponderous and opaque when they lay in shade. Of the earth it made a shifting chequer-board, as the boughs swung in the wind, and what was dazzle turned to gloom. This was no wood. It was a ballet, where light danced with shadow.

I won't say that I started out for these magical woods that morning expecting to find chair bodgers. They are not to be found for the looking. Like all the good things of this life, discovery must come unexpected. How does one find a four-leaved clover? Hunt for it over years, and it will elude you; but one day, when you have forgotten about it, there it is, at your feet. And so, with chair bodgers, you may search these woods, feeling certain that you know where they were a month ago; but they will have disappeared, leaving behind them no intimation of their new whereabouts.

I was looking at the startling beauty around me, when above the rustle of my own feet in the dead leaves I heard a distant sound of the chopping of wood. I listened carefully, for this sound was ill-matched to the season. May was no time for the wood cutter. Could it, I wondered, could it possibly be chair bodgers?

I listened again. Once more I heard the noise of chopping. This time there came with it the purr of the saw. I turned in the direction of these sounds.

Sight soon confirmed the tidings that had reached my ears. The floor of the woods was dotted with wigwam-shaped piles of beech brushwood – bavins, as the country people call them. They gave a strangely uncivilised aspect to the woods, as though they should by rights be inhabited by savage tribes. But there was as yet nothing human to be seen. As I walked further, more and more wigwams stood purple among the grey trees. And then I began to notice tree trunks lying prone upon the ground. These signs assured me; for the chair bodgers follow in the wake of the wood cutter, like gleaners in the harvest field.

Suddenly, among the heaps of brushwood, I noticed a small erection of discoloured thatch, shaped like two playing cards that had been placed against each other. It was the chair bodgers' hut. I had tracked them down. There, before me, stood the most primitive of workshops. At the base of the thatch, the walls of the hut were formed by the shavings from the bodgers' craft, increasing in bulk as the work of months swelled the deposit. The floor of the wood around this erection was covered with the same pale buff shavings, as though the beech trees had by a sudden whim cast off leaves of a lighter shade. These shavings looked strangely cold in shadow against the carpet of dead leaves, but where they escaped from the shade of the hut and ran into patches of sunlight, they blazed.

As I stood and looked at the hut before me, satisfied by its shape, I found myself thinking of the form of other buildings I had seen, and wondering why they had given me this same emotion of pleasure. And then I realised that they had one main thing in common; their form was unembellished and determined by use. In memory I was back in America, excited by the austere form of the tobacco barns of South Carolina; I was looking at the clean shapes of New England outhouses; I remembered the great grain barns of the Middle West, heaving across the landscape like big sea monsters. I thought next of the pleasure I had had from the cylinders of silos. But all these, I reflected, all these are shapes of the earth world. And before me I saw the proudly reared heads of Kentish hop oasts or Hertfordshire malt houses, functional in form. I wandered by water mills and windmills, I visited a Dorsetshire granary. And then, with the thatched hut of the chair bodgers before me, I thought of the beauty of hayricks. All these buildings and erections, I decided, are rooted in the earth and constructed for work. There is in them nothing false. Without seeking it, their builders have given rhythm to the lines and balance to the proportions.

I went nearer to the bodgers' hut. A regular vibrating sound issued from it, interwoven with a murmur of voices. From time to time a more brittle noise broke into these quiet sounds, as a turned beech wood chair leg was thrown from an opening at the side of the hut. It lay there, on the growing pile of its fellows, looking naked and incongruous against the background of dead beech leaves.

As I reached the hut I felt that I was looking at a museum piece. It seemed impossible that here and now, in the nineteen thirties, a mere six miles from one of the biggest centres of the furniture trade, this primitive craft could hold its own against the factory-made goods of the town. For here, in the shelter of a thatched hut, with a pole lathe that each generation had repeated through many centuries, two men sat from half past seven in the morning until half past seven in the evening, turning chair legs, three dozen to the hour. I must be looking at something in a glass case, labelled and catalogued. But no. There, before me, worked two flesh and blood human beings, an old man and a youth.

I thought how calm and satisfied they looked, with none of the harassed strain of the factory worker on their faces. Was this, then, the way to live and work? Did the beauty of the woods around them, and the sense of direct craftsmanship, balance the long hours at their trade? And how long can they survive? I wondered. The old man will carry his values and convictions to the grave; but his helper is young and soft and the impress of the town will not be long in stamping him. I looked from the old man as he stood at the primitive lathe, working the foot treadle that vibrated the wooden poles stretching out from the hut, to the younger one as he sat on the shaving horse, shaping the chair legs in readiness for the lathe. Neither nagged at his work, but I wondered for how long the old man would keep his companion.

Over the old man's shoulder tossed the beautiful shavings, cool and pale in colour, curling and twisting in shape. Out of the opening in the hut were flung the turned, grooved chair legs. And the young man fed the older one with the shaped wood, splitting it roughly outside, with tree stump for block, sawing it to the exact length, rounding it. Their world about them was banked with logs and tree trunks, and cluttered with chips of wood and shavings and hatchets. Three tree stumps were covered with sacks, to be used as seats when meal times rolled round. Reflecting that there were but two of them here, while places had been set for three, I remembered a talk I had had years before with an ancient chair bodger. 'We do always lay a place for a stranger,' he had explained. 'You never can tell but what the hurdle maker, or the bavin binder or one of the wood cutters mayn't pass by, and you'd be feeling bad if it looked as if you hadn't expected him. So we always lays for three.' Over a smouldering wood fire hung a kettle, suspended from an iron rod that was attached to another tree stump. It was nearing ten o'clock, the hour of their first meal, and the kettle smoked.

Once I had found my chair bodgers, I knew where to look for each of their tools. Chair bodgers are ritualists; their habits do not change. The grindstone would lie at the far side of the hut. I knew, too, that if I looked carefully, I should find the tiny can that they insert into the waterway of the trunk of a tree, that it may catch the rain for their grindstone. And if I examined that tiny pierced can I should see the small wedge at its bottom, that they remove when they wish to let the water drip through its hole upon the stone.

A distant church clock struck ten. Respecting their ritualism, I left

them, feeling I had no right to the third tree stump. As I walked away, the sun quivered through the trees, and the woods sparkled with light. But I recollected an oil lamp I had seen in a corner of the hut, and I saw before me woods in the clutch of winter, and an old man turning chair legs in the dark. 'It isn't all as romantic as you might think,' I told myself. 'It is not always a morning in May.'

THE FLOWER SHOW

T HEY'RE AS FINE a lot of gladdies as you'd see anywhere,' thought Sid
Watson. 'I will show them. I'll make myself show them. It don't matter
what they all say or think, they'll just have to admit I can grow gladdies.'

Sid Watson limped back to the shed to fetch a knife. He would cut his
gladioli now, early in the morning, before the sun touched them.

It was the day of the annual Flower Show. For weeks past the entire
village had watched the weather, knowing that upon its vagaries depended
their success today. Just so much sun and no more was needed for Mr.
Twining's sweet peas, just so much rain and no more would bring Bert
Cooper's lettuces to perfection: while some people had been known even
to wish for a spell of cold, that raspberries and red currants might be
checked in their ripening. And so it was inevitable that, at any village
gathering during the end part of July and early August, the main subject of
conversation should be the weather. For there was something comforting
in being able to cast the blame for any failure in human effort upon a force
as uncontrollable as the elements.

But to Sid Watson had been given none of this relief of speech. He had tended his gladioli in silence and alone, trembling at the sight of any dark cloud that crossed the skies, listening in fear to the weather reports on the wireless, watching with anguish for the sight of any slug in his flower beds.

Sid Watson was a new comer to the village. Whether it was his limp or his deformity, he never knew, but the fact was that nobody wanted to get to know him. Since he had taken over the cobbler's shop at the bottom of the lane the villagers had brought him their shoes to be soled; but there the matter had ended. Not a girl in the place would look his way. And because Sid Watson was a friendly creature, he felt lonely.

From the end of his garden he could see just the near part of the Flower Show field. The marquees were already erected and in the morning light they looked bulky and glaring against the bright green of the newly-mown meadow. He trembled at sight of them, wondering how he should dare to enter them with his gladioli. His nostrils smelt already the trodden grass and the cloying scent of massed flowers.

In the next garden he could hear Jim Berry shouting to his wife: 'Well, I'd best be digging up they taters of mine. And see as how you washes them more carefully this year, Emmie. I mind me as how you scratched some of they Red Kings last time with the scrubbing brush, so as the judges thought as how they weren't perfect and I didn't get no first prize. I'm sort of set on getting first prize this year. It's as fine a crop of early taters as I've had, though they do be so late this season that nobody didn't ought to dig them up yet, and what with the wet and the worms in them they won't keep.'

The gardens and allotments of the village were dotted now with figures, furtively digging and cutting and picking. For within each man was a feeling of insecurity until his exhibit was in the safety of the marquee. Who knows but that, at the eleventh hour, a sudden doom might not descend upon him, assuming the form of pillaging blackbird under the raspberry net, or burrowing worm among the carrots and potatoes. It would be safer to wrench these fruits from their earth or their bushes secretly, that nature might be taken unawares.

And if each man were on the defensive against the ravages of nature, so, too, was he armed against his neighbour. On no other occasion during the year did such distrust and rivalry abound. Neighbour against neighbour, and village against village, each man grew suspicious.

But the smaller rivalries of neighbour and village were as nothing compared with the feud between hills and plain. Never did the dual organisation of primitive societies separate two moieties more rigidly. 'It ain't never no good sending nothing to the Show until they do give us one to ourselves for up here on the chalk,' old Silas Meadwell would mutter. 'Here we do be digging ourselves to death, as you might say, to make something come out of the ground, and down there in the plain, Bledwick way, you ain't needing to do nothing but show your black earth to a seed and it do sprout before your very eyes. Is it any wonder that they do carry away all they prizes?'

But at the same time, in the bar of the White Horse, at Bledwick, Jack Potter would be grumbling about his gooseberries. 'You can't never grow a gooseberry down here on the plain same as you can up on the chalk, try as you may. And what I say is, it ain't never no good sending a gooseberry to the Show while they do let it be open for they folk in the hills. You can't wonder that they do take all the prizes for the gooseberries, now can you?'

It was shortly after nine that the first exhibit was brought into one of the empty marquees. Slowly and dramatically Joe Gaybird unpacked his hamper and counted. There they were, the eight distinct kinds of vegetables: six short carrots, twelve pods of broad beans, four globe beetroots, a pair of vegetable marrows – but at this point Joe Gaybird left off counting, that he might once again admire his marrows. He was as yet alone in the tent, and dared thus to step away from his vegetables, fearing no wilful disturbance. He walked back and back, till he reached the entrance of the marquee, that he might regard those marrows from a long way off. Somehow you couldn't seem to be able to take them all in, when you were close up against them. They overcame you. Not for nothing did Joe Gaybird have the name for the best marrows in miles around. Some said it was the black dirt of Bledwick what did it, but Joe Gaybird knew better. Let them think what they pleased, he knew it was because he cared for they marrows of his'n that they did grow so mighty like. Nobody had no right to say that plants didn't know what you were feeling about them. . . Looking round to see if he were still alone, Joe took a tape measure from his pocket and returned to his hamper, to encircle once more the girth of his marrows.

The marquee now was filling up. The white paper pinned to the tables became hidden under onions and cabbages, beets and beans.

Here, in abundance, lay foaming cauliflowers and frilled savoys, large cos lettuces and peas. But of all the vegetables that were being set out perhaps the plates of potatoes were the most conspicuous. Scrubbed

clean of every particle of earth, these pink-flushed tubers looked almost indecent in their nakedness, till you felt ashamed of being seen looking at them and turned with confusion to the carrots. But, like most of the other root vegetables, they, too, looked undressed in their scrubbed state, and in the stiffness of their arrangement were as characterless as the labouring man on a Sunday. Each – both carrot and parsnip and ploughman – needed a film of earth as raiment.

The grass underfoot spread like a thick pile carpet, deadening all sound. A hush lay upon the great tent – the hush of concentration. The face of each man, as he balanced turnip against savoy, or moved a row of peas further forward, was serious and tense. There was a sacramental feeling in the way he handled these fruits of the earth, as though he were a pagan priest at a solemn ritual of fertility. Never, outside the marquee of a village flower show, was bean pod touched with such tenderness or lettuce scrutinised with such devotion.

Throughout the hours of the morning, pea and scarlet runner were arranged and rearranged, the design of each pattern filling the minds of the men with the discontent of the artist.

But if each exhibitor was silent in his preoccupation, the swelling stream of onlookers kept up an unbroken murmur of comment.

'Looks to me as if it don't be going to be much of a show this year,' muttered Ted Wooster. 'Now, in my garden, blessed if I ain't got broad beans a sight longer'n your'n. Mine be sixteen to twenty inches long. I knows that, for I measured them only last night, I did. Sixteen to twenty inches long, they broad beans of mine be.'

Joe Gaybird was flicking imaginary bits of dust off his beets, but he turned now to Ted Wooster in contempt.

'What's the good of having bigger stuff if you haven't the courage to enter it,' he snapped. 'Why don't you show they broad beans of your'n, I asks you, so as us folks as can't grow no big stuff can see them, and measure them, and know what broad beans can be?'

But Ted Wooster was not to be outdone.

'You ask me why I don't show? And what be I going to let everybody see what I grow in my garden for? A fellow's got a right to keep some things to hisself and I reckon I don't mean to let on as to what I grows and doesn't grow. That's between me and my own dirt, as you might say.'

He moved off to another corner of the tent, to pester someone else. 'And I had to dig up a whole barrow load of carrots before I could get enough decent unsplit ones to show. It be this wet summer what have done us all in, it have. Never have I knowed such a year.'

Old men grumbled about the weather, shaking their heads as they pointed to the vegetables. And as they grumbled and compared notes, so they demonstrated the legendary size of their unexhibited produce, measuring them upon finger and arm, till it looked as though they were speaking a sign language.

Into the vegetable tent slipped Sid Watson. He had cut his gladioli, and they waited in vases, at home – waited until he should have the courage to bring them to the show. 'Better have a look round first,' Sid had decided. 'Better see what sort of a chance they've got. Better watch and get to know what other folks do, so as I can walk in with them all natural like just as though I'd done it all my life. Don't see why I should give them the opportunity to laugh at me and say it was plain I'd never brought anything to a flower show before.' He made his way round the vegetable tent, looking with envy upon the calmness of Joe Gaybird as he arranged his exhibit.

But just as he was coming out from the tent he knocked against a clump of people to the left of the entrance. With terror he saw that it was Mrs. Beedham from the Big House, surrounded by attendants and show officials.

'Let me see, where is that twelfth pea pod? 'she was asking.' Didn't we bring twelve, Simmonds? I felt sure we did. I need it for my design. You must go back to the house and fetch one.'

As she stood there, parting the crowd into two social sections, Sid moved back to join his own people. They were talking among themselves. Gladly would he have joined in, telling them of his gladioli; but they had no need of him. He was a new comer. He did not belong.

'Perhaps it's only among the vegetables that they're all so unfriendly,' thought Sid, pausing before a brilliant exhibit of tomatoes: 'I'll make myself go into the main marquee. After all, it's there that I've got to bring my gladdies.'

Timidly he slipped into the great tent, daring hardly to look about him. The morning was drawing on, and as more and more cut flowers were brought in, the place took on the appearance of a large piece of half-finished embroidery. Marigolds and dahlias and gladioli looked as though stitched in bright silks and wools against the canvas of the tent. The women and children, moving about in their gay summer dresses, seemed like bigger masses of embroidery that had become detached from the canvas background. They came and went, fetching rain water for their exhibits, bending down to unpack clothes baskets of flowers, stepping backwards to admire and criticise their floral arrangements. As they moved and bent, their coloured frocks caught the sun that slipped in through the holes and joins in the canvas, and over pink and blue of print fell stripes and freckles of light. After the sombre earth tones of the vegetable tent, the colours here seemed richly vivid.

But it was not only the massing of flowers that Sid saw in the main marquee. Here, the seasons were telescoped: rhubarb and currants lay with apples and pears. Here was not one climax but many, scattered not sparsely over the weeks, but crowded on this one day; the moment of some fruits was hastened, the time of others delayed. But not even the will to

precipitate had managed to ripen the greengages. 'It's a wicked shame to pick them as hard as this,' said Mr. Thursby, shaking his head. 'But there you are, it's got to be done.' And tenderly he arranged a dozen large green bullets on a white plate.

It was with a shock that Sid Watson looked at his watch and realised that it was past eleven o'clock. His gladioli waited still at home, in vases, their destiny as yet unsettled. Sid walked towards the cut flowers, to look at rival gladioli. And there they were, measly, skimpy things, not a spike among them as fine as his. He thought of his blue Ave Maria, erect and proud on its stalk, and his mind was made up. Bumping against people in his hurry, he rushed from the marquee to his home and fetched his flowers. It was getting near to half-past eleven as he arranged them in glass jars on the bench.

In the bustle of the tent, that morning, where the grass muted every footstep, there was one part that was left solitary and colourless. At the far end, past the array of heads of carnations, lay the plates of boiled potatoes, and the pies. Satisfied by recent breakfasts, the people had hurried past these foods with a feeling of distaste, finding the smells unappetising and repugnant. It was only at twenty-five minutes past eleven, just before the tent was closed to the public for the judging, that the school children drifted in that direction, surrounding the foods, as they gorged in imagination upon apple pie and fruit cake. But Stella Thatchcock missed the cakes and pies. Of all the enormous bunches of wild flowers that the children had that morning brought to the show, hers had been the biggest. It stood in the centre of the table, flaming forth from its tin bucket. Stella felt triumphant. She had collected sixty-three varieties. Jimmy Lucas, with all his bragging, had found only fifty-eight. But Stella could not spell. 'Why will wild flowers have such hard names,' she thought. 'I can't spell not half of them. What's the good of me getting all these kinds if they've got names as is too hard for me!' With her stump of blunt pencil she wrote down a jumble of letters, meaningless both to herself and to any judge. As she looked up at her blaze of flowers, she sighed. But at that moment a kind lady passed. 'Please can you tell me how to spell toadflax?' Stella dared to ask. They went through the list together. But time was against her. They had only reached the twenty-third flower when the tent was cleared for judging, and Stella's list remained incomplete.

It was no easy matter clearing the tent for the judging. Time after time did Mr. Piggott walk the round of the benches, shouting, begging, commanding the people to go. But they could not tear themselves from their fruit or flowers. Twice did Len Goodchild turn to leave his roses, but twice was he forced to come back to take a last look at them. It was as though they could not trust the flowers to behave themselves unattended before the judges. There was a maternal smile on Miss Glover's face as she gave a final caress to her sweet peas. So would a proud mother smooth the dress of her little girl as she sent her off to her first party.

But it was Sid Watson who suffered most. He stood in front of his gladioli, unable to move. Close to his ear came the order to leave the tent, but he did not hear it. He looked in wonder at the beauty of his Ave Maria, produced by him with his own hands on his own soil. It seemed to appeal to him not to forsake it. Never did lover tear himself from loved one with greater difficulty than Sid Watson in leaving his gladioli. But Mr. Piggott was touching him on the arm. 'I'm very sorry, Mr. Watson, but you've got

to go. The judges are waiting.' With dragging, lingering feet, Sid left the tent in a daze, remarking nothing as he passed.

A great silence fell upon the emptied marquee, broken by occasional murmurs of the 'foreign' judges who had arrived from distant villages. 'She should have purled round,' said a shrill female voice from the knitting section. 'To my mind these are better than those,' decided a heavy growl from among the Cut Flowers.

But Mr. Honisett judged the cakes alone. If they wanted his opinion – him what had the name of being the best baker in forty miles around – they'd have to let him do the job by hisself. He stood in front of the cakes and pies, slashing them in half with the large knife held in his better hand, which happened to be his left. His bowler hat lay on the back of his head and with the bottle of beer sticking out from his pocket, he looked an odd creature. 'They don't know how to make cakes these days, they don't,' he muttered to himself. 'Seems as how there ain't nobody left as can make a cake but me. When I mind me of they cakes I did make twenty year back when flour was flour and currants was currants, and there weren't no hurrying around to get your baking done quick so as you could go out to the pictures'.

Mr. Honisett stood and mused before the cakes, till the minutes passed and he was baking, twenty years back, while cakes and pies before him lay unjudged.

There was little dinner eaten that day. Minds that were occupied with the destiny of broad beans or roses were ill-attuned to the thought of food.

'Even as I am cutting up this bit of meat,' pondered Joe Gaybird, 'even at this very moment, they may be getting round to my vegs. Wonder if they cabbages have kept crisp. It's not as you might call it a hot day, but that tent did get fair stuffy before the morning was out.'

'I didn't like the draught that was creeping round my roses,' muttered Len Goodchild as he toyed with his stew.

'There was that wind rising so strong like, and blowing through that big hole in the canvas just up against where they'd placed me and my roses. I shouldn't be at all surprised if we was to go there this afternoon and find

'em all faded – just because of that there draught. And then if I don't get no prize it'll be all the fault of that wind. You mark my words, Lucy.'

It was a differently dressed crowd that covered the grass of the Flower Show field this afternoon, seeping into the marquees, caught into little whirls and currents. The rough working clothes of the morning had been thrown aside, and shining faces stood above stiff collars and severe suits. Characters appeared on this day that were not seen from one flower show to the next: aged men whose fallen-in, toothless mouths contrasted with the curve of their semi-circular beards; old women in stiff cloaks; dapper little figures in smart corduroys. For, though there was a sprinkling of local gentry, yet the Flower Show was essentially the day of the villager, a gathering of those to whom life meant the fundamentals of rain and heat and the feel of the earth between the fingers. The things at stake today were their things: the fruits of long evenings of work after a day at plough, when limbs and body ached with the strain of digging and calloused hands were heavy with fatigue. 'And yet,' said the retired schoolmaster, looking about him. 'And yet, though all these old people still come, it isn't the same as it was when I was young. In those days before buses and motor cars, it was the one meeting point of the whole year. It was the one chance people had from all the neighbouring villages to keep up their friendships. That was when it was held at the manor house. And the lanes for miles round would be full of the sounds of trotting ponies.'

As if to challenge the reactionary feelings of the retired schoolmaster, the loudspeaker blared out now with its transatlantic melodies. '. . . An airway ticket to romantic places. . .' it bawled in the ear of Mrs. Whittles, from the Lower Farm. Her mind was in a dreadful state of confusion. She had been thinking about her daughter-in-law's approaching confinement when she had met Mrs. Dewey, and they had talked of Mr. Dewey's rheumatics and she had promised to send along that lotion of hers that was so good; and then that horrid noisy music had said something about some cigarette-end stained with some lipstick or other, and now there was something about a ticket to somewhere and, oh dear, she didn't know if it was the heat or not, but she was getting in such a fluster and a muddle that she didn't know exactly where she was, or what she had been trying to think about. She hurried to the far end of the field, away from the loudspeaker, but it seemed to follow her, making fun of her as it shouted something about 'these foolish things.' Flower shows weren't the same as they'd been in her young days. Over there was the old schoolmaster. She'd ask him how he felt about it.

She waddled off, puffing in the heat.

It was inside the marquees that the greatest interest was centred. Along the benches, against the exhibits, stood the red, pink or white cards that denoted the prize-winners. Timidly did the exhibitors edge nearer and nearer to the tents, delaying the moment when they should learn of their success or failure. Joe Gaybird had got first prize for his vegetables, and the tent was full of his self-praise. 'Didn't I tell you as how I'd be getting it?' he boasted. 'Didn't I say as how nobody around here could grow marrows like mine!' He looked at Mrs. Beedham's exhibit, which had only third prize, and boasted again.

In the main marquee there was a crowd in front of the gladioli. Sid Watson had got first prize. Never before had there been such splendid spikes. But Sid Watson was not there, and as he sat at home by himself, he trembled at the thought of coming to the show, fearful of learning of his failure. 'I suppose I'll have to go along there some time or other,' he thought. 'For one thing, I'll have to bring those gladdies back home again when the Show's over.' But he sat on through the afternoon, hearing in the distance the blatant music of the loudspeaker and the hum of human movement.

'Well I never,' said Mr. Tidbury as he studied Sid's gladioli. 'And who'd have thought that Sid Watson, him what's always lived in a town, as they do say, would have been able to grow gladdies like this? Sid Watson? Who is he? Why, that odd deformed chap that came and took over old Bennie Alton's cobbler work when he died in the spring.

'A queer sort of a chap that don't know nobody. But coo! He can't half grow gladdies.'

Had Sid Watson been there that moment he need no longer have felt

lonely. But fear of intrusion had bitten into him, and he dared not come.

The wind had risen and the afternoon had turned grey. The people shivered a little as they stood about in groups. More and more did they drift to the shelter of the tents, till the air within grew thick and close. But the weather did not worry the children. Out in the field, near the town band, they ran races and played games; the little girls in their bright dresses, looking like petals of flowers blown suddenly across the field by the wind. In the tea tent there was silence as families ate their ninepenny tea of yellow slab cake and buns. But with the wind and the grey weather the spirit had gone from the Flower Show.

It was late in the evening that the change came. The setting sun dispelled the clouds and threw long shadows across the gilded grass. A lightness came into the air, and with it the people's spirits rose. It was the hour of the prize giving, but Sid Watson was not aware of this. He only knew that the sun had entered his back door and struck against the table where he sat thinking of his gladioli. It gave him courage. 'I think I will go along and see what's happened,' he decided. 'By the time as I gets there it'll be about the moment to bring them back home. Yes, I will go.'

It was the vicar who gave the prizes. As the megaphone shouted the name of each prize winner, a shy, proud villager walked down the field, cheered as he went.

Sid entered the meadow at the moment that Len Goodchild was fetching a prize for his American Pillar roses. And then, to his amazement, he heard his own name called:

'First Prize for Gladioli – Sidney Watson. Mr. Sidney Watson, step along, please.'

As his name was called through the megaphone, he walked forward to the end of the field where the vicar was giving away the prizes. His shadow in the evening light stretched far before him, touching the vicar's feet, creeping up the vicar's trousers. This long-stretching mighty shadow gave confidence to Sid Watson as he hurried across the meadow, golden in the sunlight. Never before had he felt such assurance. This shadow added stature to him. It was a brave, mighty man's shadow that did not belong to a deformed, limping cobbler. No more need he be afraid of the people in the village – he whose shadow had covered the whole length of the Flower Show meadow, he whose gladioli had taken first prize. As his shadow reached the vicar's face, darkening the sun-glinting spectacles, Sid Watson knew himself the hero that night at the Bear and Cross.

The vicar was congratulating him. 'They're lovely, Sid. How did you do it?' His voice came through as though it were spoken under water. A rush of emotion shook the cobbler. Nobody in the village had ever called him just 'Sid' before. But the vicar was still speaking to him, very far away as it seemed. 'I had a good look at them just now. How ever did you get them so big and so perfect?'

Sid Watson leant forward and whispered to the vicar.

'Well, sir,' he said, 'it's all to do with if you love them.'

THE CRICKET MATCH

If a stranger had happened along the village street this Sunday afternoon in August he would have wondered at the desolation around him. It was more than could be accounted for by the usual Sabbath quiet. It was as though a spell from a fairy tale had been cast upon the place, immobilising the inhabitants within their cottages. A cat stretched itself on a thatched porch. A linnet sang in a cage at an open window. But no human shadow broke the chalky white of the empty street.

Stand still for a moment, though, and listen. The crunch of your footsteps on the dry chalk road had been loud in your ears, drowning all remoter noises. Into the wrapping of silence breaks a muted sound of shouting and clapping and the abrupt impact of a bat against a ball. This, then, is the explanation of your deserted village. No evil spell has been cast upon it, no epidemic has laid it low. Somewhere beyond the clump of farm buildings, among the heavy elms, at the twist of the dipping road, a cricket match is being played.

But where? You look about you at the rolling country of hill and wood. There could be no cricket among those dips and folds. Your eye travels further, passing over the curves of the beech-covered slopes. But there, on the more gradual inclines, lie harvest fields whose stooks undulate as they follow the form of the land. As far as you can see, there is no flatness, no possible pitch. Turn the corner of the village, however, and the cheering grows louder. Follow the lane down the hill and there, on your left, stands a gaily-coloured omnibus, incongruous and urban against the heavy foliage. It must have conveyed the 'away' team. We are on the track.

The sun blazes upon the cricket field. With relentless heat it strikes the players, and makes the ball move, as Bill Wethers says, 'like a scorched cat.' The hands of the bowlers sweat, and they stoop to wipe them on the grass of the pitch. Shimmers of heat blur the outlines of the men's flannels, as the eye turns from the green of the pitch to the dazzling white. But it is not only the players who are exposed to this burning heat; the field is sparing of shade. That great line of elms, standing along one side, wastes its shadow upon the lane, and needlessly lays its purple hands upon hedgerow and stooks beyond. Only one small willow, at the far corner of the field, darkens a patch of grass towards the ditch.

It is no wonder that the pavilion is packed. Onlookers crowd the seat outside, rejoicing in the shade of the overhanging roof. Even the stuffy gloom within is preferable to that glare of sun. Always the same characters sit there by undisputed privilege. I turn to the left-hand corner of the pavilion, by the window gap, knowing that I shall see old Jumper Jenkins; and there he sits, a look of reminiscence in his eyes as he watches the cricket. It is not easy to believe the legend that gave his nickname to this ancient of seventy-nine years – never, until he was well past sixty, was he known to open a gate; always, the tale goes, he jumped it. Senile though he now is, he has not missed one match. Should you be rushed for time, it would be wise not to question him about cricket; for he keeps stored in his memory the names of the players and the scores of the matches, since the days of his early manhood. But there is no fear just now that he will talk. Today is a match of especial excitement. A London team plays the village. As well expect a man to chatter in church as suppose that Jumper Jenkins will talk while a match is in progress.

The women are less concerned with the cricket. They sit around the field, on the little broken benches, talking. About them, in the uncut grass and the clover, play their children; in the shade of perambulators lie their babies. And while the men and the boys watch the movement of each player, cheering this bowler and that fielder, they murmur among themselves in the heat, chiding a restless child or rocking a fretful baby. The cricket match to them is a club where they can meet and talk and escape their household duties. It means more to the young girls. They lie on the grass, their legs tossed behind them in the air, looking in their Sunday clothes like splashes of flowers. 'Beautiful shot!' shouts someone, and there is violent clapping. But the girls do not lift their eyes to the pitch. The 'away' team is in, and among the thick grasses beside them, lies one of their own men, magical in white. It is as though an officiating priest had left the altar to mingle among the congregation. The girls lie there, the thin material of their frocks following the lines of their bodies, curving tight at the waist, as though inviting some hand to encircle it. They gaze at the young cricketer, a look of 'come hither' in their eyes; but they gaze in vain, for he stares at the players before him, his mind centred on the mounting score.

'Out. Clean bowl.' A heavy, excited voice shouts at my side. It is Arthur Seabrook, the railwayman, and one of the champion village players. I smile to myself as I look at him, remembering the tale that goes round the neighbourhood. You will hear it any night at the Leg of Mutton, if you happen to mention his name, for the village has never really forgiven him, though it was years back. It seems that one Saturday, as they were playing a most important match, Arthur Seabrook suddenly stopped in the very middle of a run, just when the village side was pretty low, dropped his bat and ran off shouting: 'Good God, I've forgotten the train.' He had omitted to open the gate at the level crossing. The village, they will tell you, never recovered that day, though the railwayman, they will add, has since made many a century.

But what is happening now? Something dark has run across the pitch. The players stop for a moment, bewildered. It is a rabbit. Composing themselves, they resume play, but as they do so, a second dark mass hurls itself across the field, narrowly avoiding the cricket ball. It is the sexton's little spaniel bitch, chasing the worried rabbit. Failing in her search, she runs among the players, and leaps upon her master, the bowler. But the village does not concern itself overmuch. It happens too often.

Stumps are drawn punctually at six o'clock. It is on this understanding alone that the rector will allow Sunday play. And as the players put on sweaters and jackets, the church bells start to peal. But the village men loiter on the field. Pubs do not open today until seven o'clock. There is a whole hour to kill. Small boys relax the tension that has kept them rigid through the afternoon, and the women move homewards, to put children to bed and prepare evening meals. The sun is softer now, and sends the shadows of the stooks far across the harvest fields. It glows rich in the brightly-coloured fruit minerals that are all the men may drink. The waiting omnibus in the lane is in deep shade as the London team takes its leave. But the village team rests in the subdued heat of the cricket field, killing time.

It is summer dusk in the Leg of Mutton. The publican serves behind the bar in his flannels. The men in the taproom look like large miller moths in the half-light, hovering in white. And as the evening passes, the excitement increases and the long tales about cricket grow longer under the influence of pints of bitter. An aura of magic hangs around each flannelled man, as he sits among the villagers. The centuries of Jumper Jenkins and Bill Wethers and Arthur Seabrook leap. Never had the world seen such catches, such bowling. The men who leave the Leg of Mutton at closing time are supermen. Their feet hardly touch the lane. But their heads are among the stars.

HARVEST FESTIVAL

JOHNNY BENYON STAGGERED along the lanes with the vegetable marrow. He began to wish he had listened to his mother, when she had protested that it was too heavy for a boy of his age. His feet dragged now by her side, catching up to her pace with little broken steps. Each time he caught up with her, the vegetable marrow felt larger and heavier. It seemed to be hours ago that they had started for the church, and yet the steeple looked as far away now as ever. Johnny Benyon forgot the rapture with which he had clutched at the great bulk earlier that morning; he no longer enjoyed the cool smooth surface of it, tracing with his finger the stripes of dark green and pale yellow that converged and met at the base of the marrow. The beads of moisture at the cut stem ceased to interest him. It was through a mist of fatigue that he recollected his father's pride in its enormous size.

'Well, well, it be the biggest marrow that Samuel Benyon've ever growed,' his father had said. 'And that do be saying summat. And mind you see to it, Martha, that it do be put somewhere in the church where folks can't miss it. None of they holes and corners for Sam Benyon's marrow, sneaking away and hiding beneath Tom, Dick and Harry's carrots and turnips. And mind you put it so as the text do be uppermost, 'Praise God. S. B.' Did you ever see a text cut so grand-like on a marrow before, I asks you? Parson ought to be proud to have it in his church. Here, son, be you going to carry it?'

And so, of course, Johnny had had to take it.

He looked up at his mother. For several minutes she had been reminding him of something. He knew at last what it was: half hidden beneath her burden of carrots and turnips and baskets of apples, she looked like the brightly-coloured cover of last year's seed catalogue his father had given him. For a while he forgot the weight he carried as he thought of that cover. His pace grew slower and he fell behind.

A crowd had already gathered at the church gate. Sheaves of chrysanthemums, late roses, Michaelmas daisies and dahlias beautified tired old women. The scene was as if a garden and an orchard had suddenly been given the power of locomotion and moved along the gravel path of the churchyard, the black of the old women's skirts showing here and there among the sheaves as they walked, like patches of dark earth visible beneath swaying flowers.

As he neared the church porch, Johnny Benyon entirely forgot the weight he carried. A greater burden lay upon him, the burden of fear. To him church was a place where you were never allowed to do what you wanted to do; however happy you were feeling, you might never talk or laugh or dance. He shrank back and hid among the folds of his mother's dress, as he remembered with shame that first time he had been taken to a service. The music had suddenly burst out, and music to Johnny Benyon had meant dancing. And so he had danced, there in the middle of the church. He went cold now in the September sun as he recollected his mother's face when she had hurried him away.

But as he looked at the scene before him, terror loosened its hold. The strangest thing had happened. People were talking. Stranger still, they were talking quite loud, so that you could hear them right across the church. And they were hurrying about and almost running as they fetched things

from one place to another. Not only this, but the whole church seemed changed, till it looked rather like his mother's scullery, with empty jam jars and jugs of water all over the place, or the garden shed strewn with clippers and scissors and loose straw from his rabbit hutch. For the first time, the church felt friendly.

The decorating was well started. It was an hour or more since the first incongruous basketful of potatoes and carrots had been dumped on the altar steps, and already the austere building had surrendered. The window-ledges along the north side were fringed with pale-green apples and Michaelmas daisies, the dignity of the Norman font was hidden under squandered barley, till nothing could be seen of the nobility of its carving. Gradually the strong structural lines of the church were obscured by bosses and clumps of fruit and flowers. But if the form of the building was being sacrificed, the rich colour of the flowers gave it life. At no other time of the year did the church seem so homely.

There was a murmuring group of women at the altar, twisting ears of wheat into fan-like bouquets that branched outwards from the altar vases. As they arrived, these women were colourless and dull, but when they moved to fetch more ears of wheat they drifted across the shafts of sunlight that fell from the south windows, and were stroked by the blue of St. Peter's robe or the crimson clothing of Mary Magdalene, till shabby old hats became blue and crimson by turns, and dim aprons were flushed with the brilliance of the saints.

Static and passionless amidst this scurry of fluttering humanity lay the Lady Caroline Bramleigh. As she rested upon her elbow, her cold stone draperies drooping from her motionless breasts, she seemed to smile with compassion on the little women before her. Eyes that had beheld three hundred harvests could look on human effort with great tenderness. She lay on her tomb, one hand uplifted and outstretched, dominating the scene with a power she lacked on Sundays.

Johnny Benyon was always afraid of the Lady Caroline Bramleigh. But this morning, as he passed her with jugs of water for the rector's wife, his usual fear of her changed to a sudden pity. Though he could not have put it into words, it was the pathos of her immobility that moved him, by its contrast with this fluster of decorators. All he knew was that she looked lonely, and that he wanted to bring her within the magic circle of the harvest festival. He would quicken the dead stone of her body with the glow of flowers. He darted from one clump of women to another, stealing from them here a flaming dahlia, there late roses, that he might decorate his cold, still lady. In the rigid curve of her outstretched hand he placed an apple; against the edge of her tomb he plaited quivering oats: she lay there, wreathed in flowers.

But while Johnny had been decking the Lady Caroline Bramleigh, colour was flooding the grey church. The annual tradition was strictly followed: the altar, the font, the pulpit took precedence. The women of lesser importance were covering the window ledges and filling the odd corners with potatoes and beetroots. Automatically, and without resentment, each fitted into her place, forgetting herself only occasionally to grab at a particular flower she fancied, careless of who had brought it. The flowers by then had become public property.

Johnny felt happy, and there was triumph in his happiness, the triumph of fear overcome. Not only had he run and talked in the church, but, at the bidding of the rector's wife, he had fetched for her jam jars from the belfry, and had dared – yes, actually dared to touch one of the hanging surplices.

He recollected the terror he had felt as he looked at that row of ghosts, with their odd smell. And yet now he had touched one.

But how could you be frightened in the church this morning? There was he with the other children sitting astride the pews, and stepping over from one seat to the next. Inside him he held tight the memory of that venture into the pulpit. He could smell still the mustiness of the old hassocks. By standing on a pile of them he had managed to peep over the edge of the pulpit itself, and to imagine that he, Johnny Benyon, had been preaching. Little did all those women know, as they sipped their mid-morning tea furtively in the belfry, that he had grown up and preached to the whole church beneath him, peopling those empty pews from his imagination. His triumph fed upon itself, and he looked about him for fresh audacities. His eye fell on the lectern, but so elaborately was it decorated that he

dared not go near it; like offerings to some heathen bird-god, marrows and pumpkins lay piled at its foot, and the impassive brass eagle emerged, phoenix-like, from the smoke of twisting old man's beard.

The late September sun blazed that morning into the church porch. It glared so ruthlessly upon the marigolds and the red dahlias that one was forced to turn one's eyes away, as though one had been gazing into the heart of a fire. It lapped the cool church with little hot waves, bringing in with its tide butterflies and booming bees. It stroked the baskets of apples that arrived throughout the morning, till they felt warm still against the stone floor. The village children, almost hidden beneath sheaves of sunflowers and Michaelmas daisies, seemed to bring with them flecks of the sun into the church. For this one day all barrier between church and earth had dropped, till there was nothing discordant or wrong in the blue bottle that buzzed across the altar cloth, or the mess of torn flower stalks and crushed brambles that littered the aisle. It seemed fitting that leaves should be sticking to the skirt of the rector's wife, and that the rector himself should be stringing onions for the centre of the window in the children's corner. For this was a ceremony of the earth, more ancient than any creed. Gone for today were sin and shame and doctrine; in their place, a pagan worship of sun and earth flowed in from hills and fields, warming the cool grey of the fourteenth-century building. As this sense of earth and sun was transmuted by the church into festival, so in its turn the festival transfigured the world outside, till Daniel Burfitt, thatching a rick the other side of the churchyard wall, knew with pride that his rick was included in the ritual, and that men gave thanks for the corn he had sown and reaped.

And now the church was beginning to smell more and more like a market-place. The usual forbidding odour of village church, part dampness, part old wood, part stale gas light, was swamped by the weekday smells of apples and onions. The stinging scent of autumn flowers overcame the mustiness of old hassocks; potatoes and beets dominated the smell of prayer books and bibles. In their work clothes, even the women brought none of the usual Sabbath atmosphere of kid gloves and moth balls.

But among this gathering of women, there was one who felt superior. It was old Mrs. Dawes. She looked about her with pity. This was no Harvest Festival. Little did they know what a Harvest Festival could be.

'When I was a girl,' she said to her granddaughter who was helping to clear up the mess of flower stalks and straw, 'when I was a girl, we did things properly. Why, at Harvest Festival we lined each side of the road right through the village with our fruit and vegetables and flowers. The church wasn't big enough for all we had to give and to show. And there you walked through the village with marrows and pumpkins and apples and carrots at your feet. Those were the days to live in, I can tell you. And my old man, he was that handy with the decorations. He did use to make the sheaves of wheat and barley into shapes. There was one year he made one in the shape of a sickle, and after that, each year till he died, parson did make him do it again. And in those days there'd be a loaf of bread on the altar, five or six or ten times the size of the loaves we eat. And there'd be honey and eggs and butter and grapes. Something from us all. Those were the days to live in, my gal, I can tell you that.'

Through the hours of the September day the women worked. The sun moved westward and left the chancel, where it had warmed the apples that lay there in rows. It lighted the pulpit and the tips of the pew heads, plumed with ears of the rare bearded wheat. Moving yet further, it left the south windows and flamed through the Nativity in the west, casting across the body of the church a kaleidoscope of red and blue and green. Crimson touched the cheek of the Lady Caroline Bramleigh, as though she blushed to find herself wreathed thus in flowers.

Dusk fell upon an empty church and an ordered riot of fruit and flowers.

It was the first day of winter time. It seemed odd to be going to church in the twilight – so odd that everyone remarked on it, as they gathered in clumps outside the porch. They felt almost as though the Harvest Festival had put its clamp upon the summer and sanctioned this sudden advance into the cold of winter. For there was a nip in the air, and a general buttoning up of coats. The group in the church porch was bigger than usual, and not only was it bigger, but it was different. Here, once a year, came the farmers and the ploughboys, the carters and the milkers.

'We must start really early this evening, or we'll not get our seat,' the Miss Ransoms had said as they set off down the lane half an hour before the time of the service. 'These people who just come this one Sunday in the year haven't any feelings for those like us who come all the year round.' And so the Miss Ransoms had sat in their accustomed seat, listening to the crunching sound of feet on the gravel outside and the squeak of boots as an occasional farm hand entered the church. Their ears could not quite catch the murmured talk of crops and prices.

But it was not of the service itself that each person thought as he entered the church. The feeling of possession dominated him, and his eyes searched the building for his own special offering. Several people even pointed with their fingers at their contribution. Nobody could help noticing the cloud of disappointment on Mrs. Kimber's face as she looked in vain for her prize dahlias, or fail to hear her little gasp as she discovered them at last, wilting in a corner behind a stone carving.

'And to think that I brought my very best,' she reflected. 'And all the time any old dahlias would have done.'

The service was ruined for her.

But Sam Benyon beamed. There, at the entrance to the chancel, leaning against a painted saint, was his marrow. It seemed as if the cut text, 'Praise God. S. B.,' sang louder in his ears than anthem or hymn. What did it matter that on the opposite side to his, also leaning against a painted saint, was another marrow with 'God is Love' cut on it! It was a poor, puny thing compared with his, and had no yellow stripes. Sam Benyon, at any rate, was happy.

But it was a worrying evening for Johnny. He had been allowed to come to the service instead of going to bed, and already he was feeling tired and cross. Everything seemed to go wrong. As he took his place in the pew he saw a drowsy bee crawling along the pew head. If there was anything of which Johnny was afraid it was a bee. He fixed his eyes upon that bee, willing hard that it might tumble to the ground and be stepped upon, or at the very least that it might fall asleep until the service was over. He edged further along in the pew, reaching as far to the wall as he could. But at the first roll of the organ, a flower vase on the window sill overturned, and the water trickled down the wall. He was in a fix. At one end of the pew was the bee, at the other the dripping water. With all the force that was in him he watched that bee.

And in watching that bee, Johnny missed the scene around him. He did not notice the Prussian blue of the windows change to steely black as the evening drew on and the twilight turned to darkness. He did not see the unison between the bright-coloured dahlias on the window sills and the stained glass, as though the flowers had run up into the windows and the robes of the saints had run down into the flowers. Neither did he see the hide and seek that the flickering gas light played with the apples on the chancel steps. The Harvest Festival for Johnny Benyon was the slow, doped progress of a bumble bee along the edge of a pew.

Perhaps it was a good thing that his attention was so entirely taken up with his bee, for he would else have found it hard to keep serious at the little accidents that happened around him. As the procession of choir boys came down the chancel, the sweep of their surplices knocked over a vase of flowers, sending the water over the church floor with a loud swish. But Johnny did not hear. He was deaf, too, to the rumble of an avalanche of potatoes that shifted from a corner near the font, and to the tumble of a large green apple from a window above Mrs. Bolden's head, where it alighted on her hat. Fortunately her whimper of panic coincided with a loud passage on the organ.

It was during the sermon that Johnny suffered most. For some reason or other, the bee seemed suddenly to wake up and grow more lively. Johnny's hopes rose. Perhaps it would fly away. But all it did was to walk along his part of the pew and settle itself on his hymn book.

With his mind on the bee he did not hear the old parson deliver his message of Harvest Thanksgiving, or know that here, tonight, each man felt that message to be intended directly for him; farmer, ploughboy, carter, each knew himself to be especially glorified in his labours, and each sat with pride in his pew, reliving in imagination the cycle of the year that had culminated in this night.

'Johnny,' whispered Mrs. Benyon, 'why don't you find this hymn? Here, give me the book.'

But Johnny had escaped into sleep.

The world outside was black. The people groped their way through the churchyard, hindered rather than helped by the thin, localised gleam from the church porch – a gleam that made the mounds of the graves into mountains, and threw unexpected shadows across their path. But as they reached the lych gate to walk home through the country lanes, the clouds parted and displayed for their guidance a full harvest moon.

THE HORSE SHOW

THE PLACE SEEMED CHANGED. But there stood the familiar hills. Thanks to them one was certain that one had not strayed into an unknown district. Yet as the hills were lost from time to time in the deep mist of the rain, even that certainty grew dim. What was it that had happened?

For the quiet road on the outskirt of the little town was clogged and choked with cars. Strange police controlled the traffic, abrupt and ill-tempered in the wet heat of the September day; they were impatient with all who passed, respecting nobody. 'And who do you think you are?' Stanley Peabody swore back at them. 'I've lived here, in this place, pretty nigh on eighty-five year, and nobody ain't never stopped me from walking along my own road. 'Pass along, please!' And why, I asks you?'

The unending line of cars, horse boxes and show animals pushed Stanley Peabody close against the hedge, and blocked his passage. But even here, in the shelter of the hawthorns, tranquillity was not possible: to his right, with pictures propped against the weeds at the foot of the hedge, sat a pavement artist, caught up and brought along in the tide of the urban invasion. Stanley Peabody looked all around him, but he could not escape. He glanced in curious disgust at the chalk drawings of loaves of bread and bunches of flowers, swans on lakes, and sailing ships.

It was cruel of it to be so sopping wet today. On this everyone was agreed. The rain had started during the night, and in places the grass of the show-ground was already hidden under pools of water, reflecting the heavy dull grey of the sky. The gatemen swore with impatience as cars stuck in the churned mud of the entrance. Vendors of fruit and ices anticipated a useless day.

But the worst sufferers were the men who tended the animals. In the early hours of the morning they had wakened to the drip of rain, as they lay in bed in obscure farms among the folds of the hills. Tom Grainger thought of Duke, whom he had so groomed and polished that you could almost see your face in the shire's great flanks. He thought of the miles to go before you reached the show-ground. He knew how thick the mud would stand in the lanes around Brampton Bottom, how blinding the rain would be after you passed the top of Stourton Hill. As he braided Duke's mane with blue ribbons and knotted his tail with straw, he cursed the weather that had played him such a trick.

'And the hair round your hocks white and pure-like, as though you'd stepped out of a bowl of cream. And it'll be a sight to see you when we get you there today, what with that mud all sticking to your legs and your body streaming with rain. Now if you was a hunter, old man, instead of a great mighty shire, what earns his living on the farm, you'd be taken to the show in a horse box, you would, and arrive there all dainty and dandy-like, as if you'd come straight out of a barber's shop, as you might say. Here, now, quiet, Duke, quiet while I do this last pigtail.'

And Tom Grainger and his shire Duke had set off along the hilly lanes in the ceaseless downpour, man and horse both covered with sacks in the endeavour to keep dry. The man walked by his horse's side, looking up from time to time to the smoothness of the great neck. He guided him carefully, that they might avoid all possible puddles. Mile after mile of drenched road brought them at last within sight of the show. But just when they turned the corner of the lane that led to the show ground, they were overtaken by a horse box. It was going at a great speed, and as it passed them it splashed through an enormous puddle, sending the muddy water over Tom Grainger and Duke. They were soaked to the skin as they entered the gates of the field. The animals were grouped in the second meadow, protected from the wet by the fringe of great chestnuts. Tom Grainger and his shire were not the only ones to have suffered. Beneath the shelter of the trees men cleaned their cows, bending over hindquarters, stooping to wash mud from leg and udder, stepping back as they drew cloths along the length of swishing tail. And as the cows were cleaned, the large bodies shifted the weight from leg to leg and the eyes stared into the darkness of the chestnut undergrowth. There was a feeling of peace among the animals.

Tom Grainger tied Duke to the fence, in line with the other shire horses. He washed the mud from his legs, and combed the white hair on his hocks. His movements, in bending down to clean the horse, were slow, attuned to the world of animal and plough land. And as they tended the horses – he and Jim Webster and the new farm hand from Morland's over Hughenden way – they seemed part of the earth itself, and the lines of back and neck of the mighty shires repeated the lines of the distant hills.

A rhythm ran from horse to hill, and caught up in its sweep Tom Grainger and his bucket of water; it eternalised man and horse and mud. Here, this morning, among the animals, nothing was discordant.

It was an abrupt shock to walk from the peace of the chestnut meadow to the front part of the Horse Show. If the Village Flower Show were the great social leveller of the year, the Horse Show dug a blatant social cleavage. The difference that separated the heavy lines of the shire horses from the delicate, spare grace of the hunter spread from horse to man, and isolated the flowing tranquillity of Tom Grainger from the taut handsomeness of the aristocrat. While each kept to his separate meadow, there was no meeting point.

Handsome the aristocrats most certainly were, as they paraded the show ground with proprietary step and jerky talk. The well-made faces spoke of a life of wealth and ease, the assurance of their bearing told of the habit of command. But with all their fineness of clothing and bony structure, they yet had drifted from the earth, and it was with spiky discord that they stood out upon the show ground against the quiet curve of the hills.

Tom Grainger, with his stumpy figure and shabby overcoat, had the greater understanding of the eternal values.

But if the Flower Show belonged, essentially, to the villager, the Horse Show today was dominated by the aristocrat. Eddies of chance would sweep the world of the animals across that of the 'county,' as cows or bulls or horses were brought into the judging ring. But it would be for a brief few moments, and back to the chestnut meadow would go shire or bull. In this idle crowd they were of fleeting importance compared with hunter and horsemanship.

As the morning drew on towards midday, the gentry preponderated yet more. Cars banked the race course, in position for the afternoon's sport. With the stopping of the rain the air grew still heavier, as though sky and earth were bound together by steam. Into this close atmosphere rose and clung the hot smell of cars and motor tyres, and the odour of countless mackintoshes, subduing the scent of the trodden grass.

Tom Grainger had left Duke for a short while in the care of Jim Webster.

He had to see a man about some wurzels. He walked dazed among the gentry, seeking the root marquee.

'Whew!' he thought. 'And this is the smell of all them what has motor cars. It's enough to drive you sick, what with they rubber tyres and the petrol and all. What I say is, give me the smell of a hot wet horse or a cow as is being milked with your head against her flank. That's what you might call natural. But all these noises and shouts and smells don't suit me, they don't. Nor the women don't, neither.'

He was indifferent to the finely-cut beauty of the young horsewomen, as they strode the field in their riding habits. He was unable to appreciate the grace of their cared-for bodies or the scent of their well-groomed hair. He saw only the hard tense look in their faces and the crimson gash of their lipsticked mouths. And they, if they had even bothered to notice him, would have thought what a scrubby-looking little creature he was, with a smell of wet clothes about him. He returned to Duke and the chestnut trees and sighed with relief as he lowered himself on to a heap of dry straw.

'There's none of they hunters as comes up to you, old man,' he thought. 'They may shine and quiver and their veins do stand out like little rivers, but there weren't none of them, no, not even one of they heavyweights nor three-year-olds, what could gather at the headland as you do. They be only for show, they be. And they women too.'

But all Duke cared for was the sweet hay that lay before him, and he munched in peace.

Perhaps it was the quiet of the animals' feeding that made Mr. Hampton's bull sound so terrifying. The huge red monster puffed and roared and blew, making a gigantic noise. It was humiliating for him to be tethered like this at a show, and he seemed to know it. From time to time the rising wind blew a spiky horse chestnut upon his back from the trees above, vexing him still further. He tugged at his chain, he lowered his head to charge; but there was nothing before him but wooden palings and undergrowth. Miss Agatha and Miss Christina Mayhew were passing at this moment, enjoying the thrill of looking at dangerous animals that were safely tethered. Never before had they seen such a mighty bull so close at hand. They examined his woolly head, his heavy shoulders, silently admiring his virility. The bull felt the ignominy, and resented it. He snorted through his nostrils and gave one enormous bellow. Miss Agatha and Miss Christina Mayhew fled.

'Dear, dear,' said Miss Agatha. 'I really think one more moment and he'd have broken loose and been upon us. They're quite right in saying that you can never trust those animals. I believe he must have known you were wearing a red petticoat. They say that bulls go mad when they see something red. It must have been showing beneath your skirt. Here, Chrissie, turn round and let me have a look. And then we'll go back and see the mangolds.'

It was the time of the midday meal. The judging was over. Destinies were decided. Picnic baskets were opened in the shelter of the cars, and the gentry ate. Among the shire horses Tom Grainger and Jim Webster and the new farm-hand from Morland's also ate, sitting on straw at the

feet of the animals, or leaning against the palings. Further along, where the cattle were tethered, Andrew Rogers sat milking his judged cow. By his side stood his young wife with their child in her arms, searching among her packages for a tin mug.

'There now, that's better, Daisy, ain't it?' said Andrew Rogers. 'And it weren't my fault as I had to bring you all that way unmilked, with your udders that full that they did drip on the roads. Here, Mary, give us the mug.'

And the Rogers family sat down, also, on a heap of straw, and ate.

But Steve Duncan wanted something stronger than milk. He wanted to celebrate. He had won first prize for the best pen of three ewes, first prize for the best pen of three theaves, and second prize for his wether lambs. He hurried back from the town, bearing two bottles of beer with him.

'Come on, boys,' he shouted. 'Here's no offence meant to any of you,

but here's to my health.' The cheering from the sheep pens floated over the meadow to Tom Grainger as he sat beside his shire. He needed no beer. He hardly knew what it was he was eating. For Duke had won first prize.

So happy was Tom Grainger that afternoon, that the events of the show around him passed unremarked. He stood by the side of his shire, alert for the praise of passers-by. But they were few, and those who did walk through the chestnut meadow had mostly been there during the morning, and knew already about Duke. Not much need to tell Farmer

Lucas about it, when he'd been certain all along that Duke would get that first prize. For Farmer Lucas knew a good horse when he saw one. And as for all his friends – well, they couldn't come and see him and Duke; they hadn't got the two shillings entrance fee. He'd have to tell them all about it that night, at the Three Crowns.

No, the admiring crowds that Tom Grainger waited for in vain were crushed together in the first field, between white wooden railings of race course and banked cars. If the morning had been the time for business, the afternoon was dedicated to sport. Clapping and cheering punctuated the end of each item, whether it were riding or jumping or obstacle race. Proud frightened children rode their ponies into the ring; high-stepping, graceful yearling colts excited ripples of admiration. Lest there should be one moment's pause in the excitement, the afternoon's programme included the arrival of the local fire-engine, looking like a naming sacrificial animal at a procession. And still the large crowd cheered, and still Tom puffed his pipe in the quiet of the chestnut field, against the side of his shire.

Then the hunt arrived, and the flutter of excitement grew reverent before pink coats and hunting horn and the moving pattern of up-tailed hounds. Among the gentry stood a strange tramp-like creature; how he had arrived there, was a puzzle to the well-dressed crowd. His face glowed and his eyes gleamed and he waved his thorn stick high in the air, nearly knocking off the hats of the ladies as he did so. 'They'll be over the hill in the morning!' he shouted. The gentry turned and glared at him, unable any longer to ignore him. It wasn't done to behave like this. A mere common tramp, what right had he to concern himself with the hunt? It was their affair – they who attended each meet, who themselves rode to hounds. But to the tramp-like creature the hunt meant running over fields and through copses at the sound of the distant horn, and in his nostrils he smelt the sting of an autumn morning, with the mist hanging over the ploughed fields, and dewdrops enchaining the thorns of the bramble. He became the fox itself, chased and hunted and lost, slinking to earth at nightfall. In sympathy, his feet felt sore. But someone was touching his arm. He turned and saw a swell, who glared at him. 'You mustn't go on like this, sir, don't you know. We can't hear what's happening. Don't you know it isn't done?'

The tramp's stick fell limply to his side, and he moved off.

The rain had started again, and the parade of prize winners took place in a steamy downpour. The animals looked strangely like the procession into the ark, as they passed in varying size. Mr. Wilkin's prize sow lumbered after Mr. Hampton's monster bull, to be followed by Ted Lowrie's pair of gilts. It was Tom Grainger's moment, and he led in Duke with proud dignity, his stumpy body erect and transfigured. He did not notice the rain now, for it did not matter. Duke might get his hocks splashed till the white hair looked dappled with mud: nothing could remove the rosette of triumph. But the rain by now was falling so fast that it thinned the crowds, who ran for shelter to the surrounding marquees. Tom Grainger never knew that he led Duke round the ring before a preoccupied audience. He walked beside the horse in a state of exaltation, his feet mechanically following in the tread of the three wether lambs before him, his eyes gazing in pride at the glossy neck above him.

There was no point now in staying any longer. Gradually, as the afternoon wore on, the animals in the chestnut field melted away. The sheep and pigs disappeared into the vans under the fringe of the trees. But they left the field unobserved, for the rain had lifted and the people had gathered once more round the ring, where the jumping was in progress.

But as the animals left, it was a chance for those in the road outside the show. Throughout the day, in rain and heat, a crowd had stood at the entrance to the fields, feeding with excitement upon every stray happening. And now, as pig and cow and horse filed out, they noted each prize winner.

'Coo! There goes Steve Duncan with his sheep. Wouldn't I 'arf have liked to have seen the judge's face as he looked at they ewes of his'n. And to think as I helped feed 'em and as I did the shearing of 'em, and all for the blessed two shillings as I can't afford, I has to stand here instead of watching them be judged.'

Along the hilly lanes, at dusk, clumps of animals might be seen going home to obscure farms among the folds of the hills. And this time the farm hands do not scruple to ride the horses, as they dared not on their way to the show in the morning. For their destiny now is fixed. It is slow work, reaching home, for the lanes are narrow and twisting, and the horses have continually to be moved to the ditch, against the hedge, to give place to overtaking cars that carry the owners of the hunters, or to horse boxes containing the hunters themselves. But the cars move so quickly that they have all passed while Tom has as yet another mile and a half to go. The rain wets the bright blue of the ribbons that deck Duke's mane, and drips down Tom Grainger's neck. Man and horse are tired and wet, but as Tom jumps to the ground to open the farm gate, pride banishes fatigue.

THE PLOUGHING MATCH

THERE WAS DRAMA in the flat field. Among the slopes of the hills it lay sudden and compact. It might have been placed there for the Ploughing Match. 'Table flat,' the villagers called it. 'Toby Bidmead's table field' had been its name all the days of memory.

The habitual quiet of the field is broken this morning by the jangle of horses' harness, and the drone of tractors. It is the annual Ploughing Match, a grave event. Here are none of the aimless spectators who frequent horse show and flower show. Today each man is a connoisseur; this field offers no excitement to the casual onlooker.

At first sight the Ploughing Match resembles an ocean upon which ships cross and recross. The teams as they keep to their separate furrows can hold no intercourse. So at sea do ships pass, but never meet. But no, it is not a sea. Rather is it an enormous loom. The strips of pale stubble are the warp stretched tight across it. The furrows are the woof. Their lines of chocolate-coloured silk cross the stubble at right angles. The teams are the shuttles, ten in number. Slowly they move over the field, drawing the deep-brown silk behind them. But it is not only on the earth that this design is woven. Above, in the blue sky, it is repeated. Long white clouds pass across the firmament, parallel with the stubble, and at right angles to horse and plough. So, in two elements weaving proceeds.

As the clouds move across the sky they play tricks with the light. When they cover the sun, the gloom pales the golden stubble and darkens the brown earth, but when the sun comes out it flashes on ploughshare and horse brasses. So strong is this sudden flash, that for a short moment the form of team and plough is blotted from one's vision. As the horses gather at the headland, the metal shines like a signalling heliograph. For today, when the ploughing is finished, each horse will be judged. The best-kept animal must show glittering brasses and bright harness.

Awaiting this midday judging of the horses, carts fringe the field; their erect shafts stand up like guardians of the ploughing match. They are a varied assortment, two-wheeled, four-wheeled, farm waggon, horse box, but each is newly washed and brightly painted, and each stands ready for its horse with polished trappings. On the ground around the carts lies the horses' feed, in sacks and nose bags, leaning against an array of empty buckets.

But it is the spread of roots that catches the eye. Orange and crimson and yellow, the enormous swedes and wurzels are laid out at the field's edge. Custom demands that the ploughing match should include this show of roots. They are the brightest things in the field, and emphasise the muted earth colours of team and ploughman.

There is, however, one other brightly-coloured thing this morning in 'Toby Bidmead's table field,' and that is the shepherd's hut that has been brought along to house refreshments. Into this green lambing hut, bright as sunlit pastures after rain, disappear the men. And when they disappear, they stay there a considerable time, sitting about while they drink their pints. Outside this improvised buffet, in the open, stands a round Victorian mahogany table, looking oddly indecent and wrong, as though the rest of a stuffily furnished room and the walls thereof had disappeared, leaving the table solitary and exposed. On it stand additional jugs of beer and glasses,

and a large loaf of bread. For the weather today is finger cold. Let the sun but slip behind the great clouds and coat collars must be turned up, and bodies warmed with beer and bread.

The Ploughing Match is slow and very quiet. Up and down the field move the teams, the ten ploughs with their pairs of horses. In four and a half hours two ridges, each of them eleven yards wide between stick and hole, must be ploughed. But the only change that the onlooker can notice, as the morning passes, is that the landscape grows darker as the pale stubble is eaten up by the chocolate earth.

From the distance, at the far end of the field, comes a heavy drone: three tractors are ploughing. Their quick motion looks strange against the slow stumbling walk of the horses. But they are not discordant. Only a sentimentalist would deny their beauty. As they rip the earth and turn two furrows at once, their movements are as satisfying as those of the horses. Indeed, one could believe that they, too, are animals – obsolete creatures of the dragon family. The tractor differs from the horse by its speed, of course, but even more by its behaviour at the headland. Here, where the horses twist and stumble and stop, while plough is turned and coulter changed, the tractor without hesitation describes a great full curve.

But the tractor parts youth from age. Upon the six yards of stubble at each headland cluster the younger men of the neighbourhood, appraising

each movement of the great machine, openly disloyal to the horse-drawn plough of their ancestors. If you would see and hear the old men, you must leave the far end of the field, where the droning monster rips the double line of stubble, and come back to the nodding horses. Here cluster the fathers and uncles of the young men at plough, criticising the craftsmanship before them with untempered severity.

'The land horse be too quick,' says one old man, as he watches an especially rapid team. 'That skimmer be too deep. It do interfere with the furrow,' complains another. But it is old George Gaydew, darting from group to group, who grumbles most about the quality of today's ploughing. 'My son do travel for a big plough firm, so I ought to know what's what,' he tells each listener. 'And many a prize have I won in my time, I can tell you. And what I say is, there's no good ploughing being done today on this field. Look at they furrows; there should be a good skin on a furrow. And a furrow did ought to be square, it did, five inches deep and five inches on the skin; not like they rough ones along there.' He carries in his hand a photograph of himself at plough, standing beside two great horses, against a background of ruler-straight furrows. 'That be what I call ploughing,' he explains, as he shows the photograph to the men about him. 'I remembers they days when I did use to plough at matches. They was just the same as they be these days. We did have to open the furrows ourselves, and to finish we did have to plough and open the 'cast furrow.' And we did have the same measures and all – eleven yards to a ridge and eleven yards between, and two ridges to plough. And the 'cast furrow' had to be that straight as you could rule with it. But that was ploughing, that was. Not like what they be doing today.'

The clouds thicken in the sky and the wind grows colder. Old men draw bottles of beer from bulging pockets and call to ploughman sons as they reach the headland. 'There be nothing to raise a thirst like a ploughing match,' says little Timothy Goodchild, as he hands the quart bottle to his mighty offspring. 'And you be doing grand, Tom. Steady at it I says, son, steady at it, and you'll beat your father, you will. Here, a bit of this bread to sop up that beer inside of you. There bain't no furrows today as clean as your'n. And I tells you what, son, don't you never have no truck with they tractors. They be sent by the devil, they be, to muck up the lives of the likes of you and me. They horses was good enough for me and for my father before me and his father's father before him. And where be you different from I?'

But young Tom Goodchild's gaze had turned to the far end of the field. His eyes followed the great beast that ripped the stubble, and watched with envy the small figure of the man who controlled it. And as they rested on the tractor, fatigue descended on him, and he felt his limbs stiffen at evening, after a day at plough. Acres of heavy land stretched before him, to be broken by two stumbling horses. The rain pierced the protecting sacks on his back, and turned the clods to mud. The biting wind numbed his hands, and with difficulty he kept his grip on the handles of the plough.

In this short moment, while Timothy Goodchild was screwing the stopper of the quart beer bottle and restoring it to his pocket, Tom had deserted to the enemy camp.

THE PUB

'*Yesterday upon the stair*
I met a man who wasn't there.
He wasn't there again today,
I wish the brute would keep away.'

GEORGE BIDDLECOMBE LURCHED into the taproom of the Hen and Chickens. Feet that had followed the plough since daybreak, balancing among uneven clods and gripping the slippery earth against the turn of the horses at the headland, were slow to adjust themselves to the smoothness of the taproom floor. He walked heavily, his whole weight pressed down on the wooden boards.

He blinked. After the dim light of the early autumn dusk, everything here was a blur. He crossed the room to his assigned place on one of the settles, curving round the heavy dark shapes in his path. As his eyes grew used to the shadows, the dark shapes resolved themselves into human figures, grouped about the wood fire that smouldered in the open hearth.

But they were still blurred in outline, and it was by their accustomed positions that he knew them.

'Now was it five year ago, or only four that us did have that bad frost in May?' A voice came out of the shadows, in itself as blurry and soft as the shapes around it.

''E knows it were four year back.' A deep brown sound purred from the shades at the far end of the taproom. 'It were the year that old Tom Chandler's bull did get loose and did run along up the street, it were. I mind me well it were that year, for us was out in the garden lookin' at they taters, all killed with the frost, when I did hear that uproarious noise and did see Tom Chandler's bull run right along up the street, with Tom Chandler and his missis and Bill Stacey and Joe Emsworth a-chasing of it.'

A quietness followed, frayed by the striking of a match as a pipe was relit, and the whine of a dreaming dog asleep by its master's side.

'No, no, that weren't four year back, that weren't.' A thin piping voice broke in. 'That were six year come this next May. Yes, yes, it were. I knows that well, for the day Tom Chandler's bull did run loose, us had been to market to buy that little white heifer of mine. I mind me thinkin' it were a good thing it were Tom Chandler's bull what did get loose and not my little white heifer. Don't 'e mind that, George?'

George Biddlecombe had been silently absorbed into the close circle of the taproom as a unit of its society. He grunted now.

'I don't mind me of Tom Chandler's bull, but I mind me that the May we did have that frost my beans hadn't never come up and I was a-thinkin' how lucky that were, for if they'd come up they'd sure have bin killed. I never had no beans that year. No, never had none, I didn't – though my beans be always so high, yes, so as I've had to use a step ladder to pick 'em.' George Biddlecombe was expanding. The warm air of the taproom had already dimmed his memory of the dank autumnal dusk; the soothing drone of voices had chased away the rasp of coulter against plough.

He stretched himself in his place on the settle, throwing off the tension that had stiffened him even as he had lurched into the Hen and Chickens. Had he been detached and analytical, questioning his state of mind, he would have said that here in this company of men he could be himself; here, within these closed doors he could measure his true value, could boast unchid. He would have known that he was tracing the eternal pattern of the labouring man: that pattern of ploughland and solitude by day with the interchange of drink and company by night. He would have understood that this gathering here was inevitable, governed by the law of human needs. As it was, he had merely a feeling of well-being, in which his mind forgot its preoccupations and his body breathed deeply. It did not concern him that this closest of societies, the taproom of a village pub, was the direct descendant of the men's clubhouse of primeval times. It did not bother his head that this escape from the womenfolk was no new thing, but threw back across the centuries to the days when a woman entered the men's quarters on pain of death. He only knew that it was fine and good to be away from Sue. Here you could talk real man's talk and think real man's thoughts. Here you could sit and do nothing, with no one to rebuke you.

He looked about him unseeing. Had he been less doped with fatigue he might have noticed the polish on the arms of the settles, rubbed bright by the sleeves of generations of ploughmen; he might have delighted childishly in the design of circles upon the deal table, relics of the beer mug stains of his ancestors. But all these sensory things entered into him unremarked, and he was conscious only of pleasure in the close warmth of many human bodies, bound yet closer by ropes of smoke.

In the chimney hung hams and flitches of bacon. The taproom walls were festooned with jowls and hocks. In the dark now, they hung heavy and mysterious, shapes to be divined rather than seen. But George Biddlecombe knew each one.

'That be Bert Peabody's ham,' he mused. 'And over there be Jim Pitcher's – must have bin there a good six year, it must. And up in the chimney be mine and Sue's – our flitch o' bacon.'

He wandered off down a little lane of thought, alone and secret, where he met scents and sounds: scents of hot rashers, sounds of sizzling as you come back to breakfast on wet winter mornings. Sue there; the rain dripping from your hat as you stoop to wipe your boots; young Tom crying inside; and

above it all the sound of the sizzling of bacon.

But he was jerked back from his wanderings. Something was happening to the brown gloom about him: the brown of wood and walls, of paint and beer, and men's heads and coats, even of the dogs lying around on the taproom floor. Fans of rich gold broke into the quiet dusk as Mr. Crawley brought in the oil lamp. The light struck balls of amber fire in the beer mugs and brought out here a nose and there a jaw bone, accentuating the planes of the men's faces with sharp-edged shadows. As Mr. Crawley moved across the room with the lamp to place it upon the mantelshelf, the shifting light played strange pranks with the human forms that it touched, challenging the wavering flames of the wood fire in its power to distort. Shapes that had been blurred in the gloom now leapt into prominence, throwing behind them far-stretching black masses that crept up the wall and across the ceiling. To each figure, were it in itself insignificant and puny, was added the weighty dignity of an enormous shadow, till the taproom took on the appearance of a gathering of giants.

'Well, Mr. Crawley,' said Shepherd Wayland, 'you'll be needin' to enlarge your premises soon from what I can hear tell. That new feller up at the Bull be emptyin' his place. What for do he want to go and get all respectable-like, I wants to know. It seems he don't want no common folk like us about there now. The old Bull what I did use to know be turned into a castle, as you might say. And what do we be wanting with castles? They do make us feel uncomfortable so as we just stays out of 'em. It be all the gentry what comes down to the country to live what they do call the 'simple life' that he do be playin' for. They castles be all right for them. Ted Wooster do say as he went in for a pint o' bitters and sat down to have a bit of a chat, as you might say, when the new landlord did just get up and let him bide alone, while he went off to talk to some skirt, and never so much as came back till he came to get Ted's money. Now what's the use of goin' to the pub if you're not to have a talk? If it's only the beer you want – well, you might just as well get your wife to fetch it for you, and stop at home. No, no, things do be changin' these days.'

Shepherd Wayland took off his cap and wiped his forehead. Lighting his pipe, he seemed about to speak again, but at this moment Ted Wooster himself came in. He was loudly greeted; sticks and feet thumped the floor, beer mugs and fists banged the table.

'Well, there now, if it bain't good old Ted. To think that I should ever live to see Ted Wooster come into the Hen and Chickens – him what's stood firm by the Bull all these years.'

Ted Wooster waggled his head, till his semi-circular beard trembled in the lamplight. Standing there in the middle of the taproom floor, he was enjoying his welcome. He wished to prolong it. It was good; it was warming.

'What I do be sayin' is the Bull's good enough for Ted Wooster all these years, but when they do begin to call it the Bulwer Arms, then it's time he got up and left. Bulwer Arms, indeed! If there be one thing on this earth of our'n that nobody ain't never got no right to change, it be the name of a public. Why, I mind me way back when I was a young 'un it were always by the names of the publics that we would talk about places. The carrier would stop at the Swan or the Saracen's Head or the Silent 'Oman or the World Turned Upside Down. Yes, and I do mind me of they signs we did have; they were that grand. The World Turned Upside Down did have a donkey driving a man what was in harness on one side and a rabbit shooting at a man on the other. And it were always like getting near home when you did pass that sign. But the Bulwer Arms! The Bull was good enough for me.'

Ted Wooster sat down. This unaccustomed emotion had exhausted him, and he dismissed the subject with a loud spit.

A silence followed this outburst, with intervals of a drone of voices, and then came silence again. It was an eloquent lack of talk, and a comprehended one. To enter this circle was to escape from the endless chatter of the womenfolk. It was as though each man brought with him to the common pool of quietness the silence that he had lived that day on hillside and ploughland. The rhythm of their work differed from the jerky domestic rhythm of the women's world, and it demanded this tranquillity. More even than the beer, it was this necessity that nightly filled the taproom of the Hen and Chickens. Each in her separate cottage the women sat or worked. Resentfully they were aware of the rivalry of the village pub, but only dimly did they understand. Sue Biddlecombe, Lizzie Simpson, Nan Wooster and Mary Peabody, bound together by this common desertion, yet did not share their loneliness. As the hours of the autumn evening ticked away, each nursed in her thoughts a jealousy that made of her man's behaviour a personal affront. Imagining wild orgies of drink and rowdiness, they would have been bewildered had they seen their men, George and Jeremy, Ted and Bert, sitting in a silence that was to them incomprehensible.

There are subtle shades in the quality of silence. As these men sat motionless in their custom-assigned places, puffing at pipes, drinking from mugs, the silence grew out of the soil of a warm, gentle relaxation; exhausted bodies sank deeply into seats, feet rested heavily upon the ground; arms that had held reins or beaten horseshoes lay quietly inactive.

But beneath the silence this evening at the Hen and Chickens, each man felt the movement of an unusual excitement. Something had happened – something that changed this evening from the shape of all the evenings before it. Ted Wooster had returned. Somewhere within each man's consciousness was a desire to celebrate. But it was not until Bert Peabody cleared his throat and spoke up that this excitement merged into a common desire, known to all.

'Come on, Shepherd, give us a song.'

Shepherd Wayland turned round slowly in his place.

'Somehow I can't think of no song tonight.'

'Come on, I say. Give us a song, something like 'Crawley's Ales are New.'

Very slowly Shepherd Wayland rose and even more slowly he walked across the taproom floor and went out at the door.

The men nodded and winked at each other.

'We know what that do mean. That do mean that Shepherd be gone outside to think over what he be going to sing. When Jack Wayland do go out so sudden and slow like that, it do always mean that he be wanting to think out a song to sing to us.'

It was a changed Shepherd Wayland who re-entered the taproom. A twinkle quickened his childish blue eyes, red-rimmed as though from a life of weeping. His seventy-eight-year-old body had straightened like a young tree. He stopped in the centre of the floor, his hands in his trouser pockets, one leg dramatically forward.

The silence now grew strained with expectancy. It could not last long. Something must break it. And then Jack Wayland sang.

It would seem that the song had power to throw Jack Wayland back across the years, for with the first words he reverted in accent to the old Buckingham dialect:

> 'All three haley fellows,
> Going over the hills together,
> Going over the hills together,
> To join the jovial crew.
>
> 'The landlord's daughter she came in,
> He kissed her rosy cheeks and chin,
> And called for quarts of good ale to come in
> While Crawley's Ales are new.'

As he sang through verse after verse of his song. Jack Wayland's body swayed to the rhythm of the metre, till he would lean forward first on one leg and then on the other, to give emphasis. And as he reached the chorus of each verse, the men sitting around him joined in:

> 'The next as came in was a slater,
> Lucky was he no later,

Lucky was he no later
To join the jovial crew.

'He whacked his hammer against the wall,*
He wished the churches and chapels 'ud fall,
And there'd be work for slaters all
While Crawley's Ales are new.

'The next as came in was a tinker,*
And he was no small beer drinker,
And he was no small beer drinker,
To join the jovial crew.

'He says; Have you got any pots*
Or pans or kettles to mend?
My rivets are made of the best of metal.
Good Lord how his hammer and pincers did rattle
Whilst Crawley's Ales were new.'

Verse after verse unrolled, till it seemed that the song was endless. And when it did stop, there was but a short pause before Jack Wayland sang again:

'Her hair in her ringlets hanging down...'

On and on he went, and the landlord came in unnoticed to draw the curtains. It was only when George Biddlecombe let fall his ash stick on the ground that the spell seemed to smash.

'I mind me of George's old father,' said Ted Wooster. 'How he used to stand up when we asked him for a song – a good old Buckingham song – and he'd put on his hat and spit on his hands and start off. And he'd have gone on for fourteen hours at a stretch, if the landlord had let him. And as it was, it was that hard to stop him just before closing time, for you can't stop a man in the middle of singing a song, not even if it do be closing time. I mind me how George's old father would go out at ten o'clock, and if he had a mind to, he'd sing the next song he had in his head outside. And all of us would join in the chorus and then he'd sing another, and another. There weren't no stopping George's old father once he'd started singing his songs.'

The spell was surely broken. George rose to leave.

'Well, I must be getting home. I've got work before me to-night. I've got my mushrooms to gather. I've the ladder all ready.'

As he spoke, the rich humour of the labourer played about the refilled mugs and tossed benign scoffing from man to man.

'Yes, you *would*. What'ud one expect from a fellow what's lived at Haddenham most of his days – at Haddenham where they thatches the pond so as to keep the ducks dry.'

There were hiccoughs and giggles at this well-worn joke.

'Yes – and coming from the place where they killed the donkey!'

''Ere now, that's new, Joe. Tell us who killed the donkey!'

'Why, yes – killed the donkey, as you might say, because 'e wouldn't go up and roost with the fowls.'

More hiccoughs and giggles followed.

But Jeremy Simpson was discussing the war. He was getting to the bottom of his fourth pint, and Jeremy had a bad head for drink.

'Yes,' he gurgled, 'and I turned to the sergeant and said: 'Sergeant,' I said, 'you see that row of dead Boches down there? Believe it or not,' I turned and said, 'it was Jeremy Simpson what tipped them all over.' 'Must be getting near closing time,' said an old man in the farthest corner. 'When Jerry Simpson do tell us that yarn, I always reckon it be nigh on five minutes to ten.'

FELLING TREES

TED WOOLCOTT DID NOT NOTICE the jolts as he drove his pony and cart along the fringe of the woods. Up a steep slope crawled Beauty, and the cart slid backwards in the mud, pulling the pony with it. Down another slope trotted the horse, slipping forward on the carpet of wet leaves. Round a twist in the hilly lane they lurched, and Beauty's nosebag fell across the floor of the cart, tumbling against Ted's legs. From time to time they lumbered over stumps of felled trees that were hidden from the pony's sight by layers of dead leaves. Unconsciously the man in the cart gripped its side, to steady himself at each lurch; but his eyes were not following the twists and slopes, and his mind was away in the hills among the distant beech trees.

Perhaps it was the sting of the winter morning that gave him the feeling of strength and power. The misty air whipped his face and sent the blood racing through his body. 'This be the kind of weather for me,' he had told his wife. 'None of they languid summer days when you don't want to do nothing but lay about, under the plum tree in the shade. A man can feel as he's a man on a winter day like this.'

The horse had stopped now at the lane's end. Steep before them rose the beech woods, mile upon mile of shining trunks, mile after mile of bronze carpeting. But they were hidden this day in mist. Only the few trees at the wood's edge stood out flat and dark against the dove-grey world beyond. The woodman turned his pony to graze on a patch of wayside grass, and strode among the trees.

Within him, too instinctive to be intellectualised, stirred this feeling of power. It was given to him this day to alter the shape of the countryside, to demolish landmarks that had been known to his father's fathers. He, stocky little Ted Woolcott, the man who sold firewood in the plain, would today command four strong men, and at his bidding they would fell the mighty trees. 'This one, and this one, and that grand old fellar over there, with the ivy growing up him, and that thick'un way down yonder, near they holly bushes,' he would tell the head woodman, and each tree would stand doomed by the gash of the axe. At his request, fifteen minutes would lay low a beech that had withstood the storms of eighty winters. Ted Woolcott had bought sixty trees.

He looked about him at the sound of voices. There, at the top of the slope the woodmen stood, dimmed by the mist, their paraphernalia of double saws and axes heaped like firearms at their side.

The mist wrapped the woods in silence, protecting them from all invasion of sound from the outside world. Neither lowing of cattle nor crunching of cart seemed able to penetrate the veils surrounding the trees, so that the men's voices rang clear and naked.

And then, as Ted had imagined, he was walking the woods with the head woodman, condemning this tree and that, and the thick one over by the holly bushes. A stranger this morning would have lost his way in the bewildering confusion of the fog; but Ted Woolcott knew the place of each tree, and the shape of each branch. His feet sensed the form of the ground beneath them and instinct could have guided him among the maze of trunks, though it were in the dead of night. It was not for nothing that he had poached rabbits here in his youth, and cleared the woods for kindling since the years of early manhood.

The three men had followed in the track of Ted and the head woodman, and while as yet the doom of many trees lay in the balance, the silence of the beech slopes was smashed by the cracking gash of three axes. Into the folds of the tree-covered hills the cracking sound leapt, and echo tossed it back, from fold to fold, multiplying the volume of sound, till it seemed to come, not from three axes but from a score.

Into this volley of cracking broke a duller noise. Two men knelt at the foot of a great beech, bound to each other by the length of a double saw. Into the jagged clefts they had gashed, they had laid the teeth of the saw and now, with swaying movement, they were sending the tree to its death. As they knelt there at the base of the trunk, they looked, in the muted colours of their clothing, almost like tree stumps themselves.

Though they were the defilers and destroyers of this wood, they yet had nothing alien or discordant about them. The trees and the undergrowth seemed now to include them as rightful neighbours, one with the rotting leaves and the caterpillar, the cuckoo in summer and the rabbit that had its warren in the clearings. It made no difference that they were here to massacre; the rabbit devoured the young tips of spring growth, the caterpillar thinned the leaves of the beech trees in the height of summer. All around, were it by man or rodent or insect, the woods were plundered.

The first tree was near to falling. There was no visible tremor in the trunk, but the two men were aware of stirrings in the core of the great beech. 'You hold tight, Frank, it's on the chatter already,' they warned each other. 'And I wouldn't like to say which way it do be going. It be cracking somewhere. And this'un 'ull reach further than you'd think for, by the look of it.'

With fear in their movements, the men jerked the saw from the tree and ran, hollering as they went. Anyone watching their sudden terror would have been surprised and perhaps disappointed in their lack of spirit. There had been such sureness of action in each drawing of the saw through the trunk, such conscious domination over the mighty tree. But the men knew the moment at which they gave over their mastery. They knew the

time when that great mass had it in its power to retaliate and to crush their bones as it fell to its own death. They were aware of the force with which even odd broken branches might strike, bearing down upon them from the great height of the tree tops.

From their positions of safety the men watched, studying the top of the tree, that they might learn where it would fall. And then it fell. With a shivering crack it swished past the standing trees around it, ripping off some of their topmost branches in its passage. As it fell, it drew down with it to its death a sapling ash that stood across its pathway, and ripped from the undergrowth a tangle of ivy. With an awful rumble and thud it reached the ground, and, like some great animal in the throes of death, gave one last heaving bounce before it lay still for all time.

Ted Woolcott heard the ugly noise, and in the accentuated silence that followed, he exulted in power. It was no abnormal will to power that he enjoyed, no unnatural wish to destroy. It consisted merely of a tremendous excitement in domination over nature, rising to its height at the felling of a great tree. 'It be for me that this wood do be all changed like,' he boasted to himself. 'It be for me that all they trees will lay on the ground, waiting for me to saw them up and take them away.'

He walked across to the fallen tree, regarding it with pride. So much occupied was he with his own thoughts that Ted scarcely heard the head woodman boasting of his own craft. 'I measures it with a three-foot long straight branch, along the length of the trunk, like this, I told the squire's friends.' He started to measure Ted's prostrate beech. 'And then, at exactly half way up the trunk I cuts the measurements, like this, I told them.' He cut strange hieroglyphs on the trunk, of lines and crossed lines and half lines. 'You'd be surprised at how ignorant they gents was. They couldn't even do the arithmetic of the thing, they couldn't. But there, as I says to them, we can't all know about each other's jobs, now can we? You counts the length of the tree to within two inches in thickness at the top, for firewood, I says. And then you tapes round, like this, for quarter girth for cubic feet. And didn't I catch'em out with they quarter girth measurements! They would hardly believe me when I tells them that six inches across is only quarter of twelve inches across in quarter girth, and eight and a half inches is the half of twelve inches.

'And, of course, as you go bigger...'

But Ted was no longer there, and the head woodman had been expatiating to the undergrowth around him. Away, against the far slope, had sounded another ugly thud, and one more beech lay prostrate for all time. Ted Woolcott stood and looked at this one with a little less pride. The novelty already palled.

The woods tossed the sounds about like a thunderstorm among mountains. Throughout the day, crack of axe, purr of saw, snap of branches, thud of falling tree, each sound echoed and re-echoed among the hills; but each sound accompanied a movement in the drama, as man swung the axe, or drew the saw, and tree plunged forward to its doom.

The early winter dusk fell upon mauled, trodden undergrowth, crushed by the fall of the great trees. The trunks gave to the woods the appearance of the aftermath of a battlefield in a country of giants. Silence lay upon everything. Even the air seemed quieter and more still than usual; prone branches could no longer wave and moan in the wind. The mist had cleared, and the last flicker of the winter sunset burst for the first time through the gap in the trees to the southwest. It flushed the grey trunks of the felled trees; but it could not give them life. They lay there silent and unmoving. Into this silence broke the sound of bewildered robins, seeking their homes among crushed undergrowth and bushes.

BELL RINGERS

HE SEIZED MISS LILY ROUND THE WAIST and kissed her twice – big, smacking kisses on that red mouth of hers. Lord, how he'd wanted to do this, since the first day the new Rector came to the parish with those three plump daughters. He jerked the plate of turkey from Miss Lily's hands, and pulled her down to his lap, feeling the warmth of her soft body. But just as he was going to kiss her again, on her neck and her arms and down the front of her dress that was loose as she stooped with the plate of turkey, there stood Mr. Grinter, the farmer he'd worked for when he was a young man, across Shaftesbury way; and Mr. Grinter snorted. As he stared at the heavy man before him, he saw the nose thicken and the face turn into the head of a pig. And the great looming pig came nearer and nearer to him. He tried to escape, but Miss Lily was fastened to his lap, and he could not move. Miss Charlotte leaned over the table, handing a plate of jelly to Sam Bye. 'Give us some more,' shouted Sam Bye. 'I wants some more of that thick there wobbly stuff. How do you think as I can ring in the New Year on this. It's only one bell, and I needs six.' The jelly quivered on the plate, and a deep sound came from it. 'It's odd that she can get on a dish as small as that,' thought Timothy Childs. And then Miss Florrie came into the room, carrying a large jug of beer, and out from the jug of beer tumbled the rest of the bells – one, two, three, four, five – out on to the empty plates of the bell-ringers seated around the table. 'But where's mine?' shouted Timothy Childs. 'It's I what be the captain these days. It's I what should call the peal. Give her to me, I says.'

But though Tim Childs shouted till he grew hoarse, nobody noticed him. The bells on the plates rang louder and louder, as they grew larger and then larger.

'Bob! Bob, I tell you. It's all wrong that you're ringing. It's Stedman you're at. And how do you think as you can ring Stedman on six bells?'

But no one seemed to hear him.

The Rector was standing near, a 'sally' rope in each hand. Suddenly Tim felt thirsty. There was nothing to drink. Even the jellies had turned into bells. Strange, for there used always to be so much liquor at the choir suppers. But what was the good of shouting, if no one heard you? Timothy Childs grabbed a 'sally 'from the Rector's hand and pulled. From the tufted end of the rope spurted a flow of cider, and Tim drank. It was hot that afternoon in the cowshed, and Tim thought he would never stop drinking. Nice Snowball. It was just like her. No wonder she was the pet of the whole herd. She was always so soft and gentle and kind. And how freely she let the milk down from her udders. But who'd have thought that she'd have done this? There was he, milking her on and on and on, and it was cider she was giving him, and not milk. But there, she knew he had no taste for milk. The cider grew cool and splashed upon his face, spreading over his forehead. And now Snowball was speaking to him:

'Gently, Tim. Gently, I say. It's only me, your Jane. And as I said to the Rector this afternoon, it isn't no good their expecting you tonight.'

'But your name's Snowball,' said Timothy Childs. 'Nice Snowball. Dear Snowball. And to think as how you guessed as I was thirsty.'

'It's my opinion as how you've got a fever, Tim Childs. Your forehead's that hot, it's as though it were burning. Another word about that bell-ringing tonight and I fetches the doctor. And then you know what he'll say. It'll be bed for you, right away. It's no good your going on about feeling well, when it's the flu you've got, and you know it.'

Timothy Childs opened his eyes, but everything before him was blurred. And then the blur parted, like a mist before the sun, and he recognised his wife.

'Well, there now, Jane. Fancy you coming down to help me with the milking. It's many a year since you bin and done that. I mind me of they days when I was courting you, and you'd slip down from the farmhouse and make believe as how the hens had taken to laying their eggs in the cowshed and you must needs come and look for them. And then we did look for 'em together. We didn't never find no eggs, did we, Jane? But we found something else…

'Where's Snowball gone to? I can't seem to see her nowhere.'

'You've been asleep and dreaming. That's what it is. And calling out in your sleep something dreadful. Here, now, drink this.'

The background took form about his wife's figure, till clear before him he saw fireplace and mantelshelf. At his feet on the hearthrug slept Spot. Over his knees was tucked an old overcoat. He shivered, and drew the chair nearer to the fire. It was strange how heavy that chair felt. It took all a man's strength to move it. Odd that he'd never noticed it before.

'How long do you reckon as I slept, Jane?' It seemed years since he remembered sitting here in this chair before the fire. 'All I know is as I was back in Dorset as a young 'un, that time as how I was cowman at Farmer Burdon's, and it was New Year's Eve and we was all at the choir supper at the Rectory. They was grand times, wasn't they, Jenny, with the Rector's daughters waiting on we at table, all dolled up in their pretty dresses, and handing us out they plates of turkey and beef and jellies. It was jellies as we did use to have, wasn't it? Somehow, it seemed to get all mixed up in my dream. Tell me it was jellies, Jane! And then we did sing all they songs. I mind me as how there was one particular song as was called 'Marching through Georgia' that we did turn into a part song. The Reverend Forster always set such store by his bells, he did, and treated us bell-ringers like kings, as you might say. Nothing weren't too good for us. There weren't never one of we as did ring up they bells on a dry throat. And there he did stand, though he were nigh on his three score and ten, and wish us a Happy New Year. It do seem to me, Jane, as I do feel that tired that I might have been ringing a peal in my sleep.'

Timothy Childs lay back in his chair and closed his eyes. Snow was falling, and the silence of the world outside seemed to penetrate the walls of the cottage and to flood the room, muting all sound. The clock ticked on the mantelpiece, mingling with the click of Mrs. Childs' knitting needles; but even these failed to destroy the quietness, sounding, as they did, submerged and muffled.

'If I goes on like this he'll fall asleep again,' thought Mrs. Childs. 'It's the knitting needles as always does it. And then he'll forget they bells, and I shan't have no need to fight him about it. The very idea of his going out on a night like this with the influenza upon him!'

But at this moment the church clock struck eleven. Cloaked in snow though the sound was, it roused the man by the fire. The fever rushed upon him once more, and he sprang from his chair.

'Be that ten or eleven that be striking? 'He looked at the clock on the mantelshelf. 'It's time I got going, Jane. Now then, take your arms off me, I tell you. When Timothy Childs have made up his mind to do a thing there ain't nothing on earth what will stop him, least of all a woman's fears. Here, now, where's my woollen jersey?'

Mrs. Childs knew herself to be defeated, but still she clung to him. 'It's the fever what be making you like this, Tim. You don't have no idea what you be doing. And it's not as though I didn't go and tell the Rector this very afternoon that you wouldn't be coming.'

'Don't know what I be doing! Me! The captain of the bell-ringers! And with John Drury and George Goodchild down with the flu, and nobody extra to take their places! The New Year've got to be rung in properly, it have. I tell you, there ain't never been a time since I was a young 'un that Timothy Childs haven't rung in the New Year, and he'll be doing it tonight.'

He wrenched himself free of the woman and lurched from the room.
The snow silenced his footsteps as he walked down the path. All that Jane
Childs could hear was a creak as he lifted the latch of the garden gate.

The bell-ringers stamped their feet and beat their arms. The church
struck damp and cold. It was as though the stone of the walls failed to
isolate them from the bitter weather outside, and flakes of snow penetrated
it and were changed into rivulets of icy sweat, that trickled from one stone
to the next. The men's breath was visible in the air before them. Even the
gaslight smelt fungoid and clammy, and the warm red of the holly berries
that decorated the church mocked the midnight invaders.

'It be just nigh on half past eleven,' said Philip Spittles. 'I reckon as we'd best be starting. The Rector says as how we can't be sure of Tim Childs to-night. His missis is keeping him at home with the 'flu. But if I knows Timothy Childs, she isn't half having a time with him. Come along, boys. It'll warm us up anyhow.'

The five men scrambled up the stone steps to the belfry, numbed still with the cold. With dead fingers they unbuttoned their coats, and flung them in a pile on the floor. Blowing on their hands, they seized the sallies, eager to begin. Behind them, on the walls of the belfry, stood five black giants, grasping the ends of gargantuan ropes.

But at this moment the ringers heard the whine of the church door. With the haste of fever, Tim Childs leapt up the twisting steps, and burst upon the five men, his eyes flaming.

'That be my bell, the tenor, Phil Spittles. Here, give her to me. And did you all think as how Timothy Childs wasn't going to ring in the New Year? And you knowing me this long time!'

The bells crashed upon the silence of the church. Their sound floated over the snow-covered hills, and slipped into bedrooms, stirring the sleepers from their rest. Annie Drury slid from her bed and closed the window, that John might not waken and grow restive. 'This be the first time since we was married as he haven't been able to ring in the New Year,' she thought. 'And if he was to hear they bells I wouldn't say as how he mightn't get out of bed with the flu on him, and all.' She pulled the coverlet over his ears, to deaden the call.

Mrs. Wheeler lay huddled in her great bed. Under the weight of her blankets she shivered, beating off the sound of the bells. But they were relentless, and shattered her peace. She wriggled to the edge, to withdraw herself from the ghost that lay beside her. 'Tom!' she screamed. 'Tom!' The bed was wide and cold. 'For thirty-six years we listened to them together, you and me. And you would always turn in bed and kiss me as the New Year came in. And now you'll be hearing they bells so loud, just above your head.'

The six figures stood in the belfry, and the six ropes slid upwards from their grip with a sense of release. Behind them, the six black giants loosened hold on their ropes, and tugged them down again, endlessly and with ease. The men talked and joked as they rang, rising on tiptoe with the spring of the rope, lifting their heads to the darkness above them. The feet of the black giants lay spread on the ground about them, tying one figure to the next, and making of the six men a unity.

But though Timothy Childs was one with the bell-ringers in body, his fevered mind danced with the heavens. Boom, went his great tenor bell. It was the stroke that was to kill the old year, smashing it across the path of the stars. 214356. 241536. 425136. Boom! Boom! Boom! The old year lay writhing in agony, and he, Timothy Childs, rope in hand, dragged its dying body along, among the clouds and the hills. With each tug at the sally he heaved the year further and yet further from the heavens. As he felt its weight at the rope's end, he looked up and saw it, a great red dragon, having seven heads and ten horns and seven crowns upon its head. And in the air about it were lightnings and thunderings and voices, drowning the death rattle of the old year itself. But it wouldn't die. It cried into the night, a cry that changed and kept changing, and then repeating itself; but always a cry. Timothy Childs pulled yet harder at the rope: 'It shall die. It must die. It's got to die. And it be I who've been sent to kill it, I with a sword in my left hand and in my right hand seven stars. It've got to be dragged down to the earth, till it do lie silent and still among they beech trees in the woods over Hampden way. And the old year fell unto the earth, even as a fig tree casteth her untimely fruits, when she is shaken of a mighty wind. But that be wrong. There bain't nothing untimely about his death – him what did leave Ebb Stopps to get destroyed by a motor car, till his body lay crimson in the road with blood; him what hardened the Rector's heart till he turned little Amy Simmonds from the Rectory because that she did grow and swell, like they marrows that is sent by Almighty God. There bain't nothing good to be said of it – it' as sent us a drought to kill our flowers, and the consumption to poor Emily Stacey, and a bad potato harvest. Lord, it be dying. It be dying at last!'

'Have you forgotten to look at the clock?' A sharp voice sounded at his side. 'It be just on midnight. And it's you as is to ring in the New Year, Tim.'

Silence fell upon the belfry. 'It be dead at last,' sighed Timothy Childs. 'It be quiet, and cries no more.'

He tolled the twelve monotonous strokes of midnight, the death knell of the old year.

But he did not hear the greetings about him. His task was not yet done. The New Year waited for him, shy and young, and he must attend her.

'I am the bright and morning star,' he murmured. 'And it be I as must bring her in. Behold I make all things new. And I must show her to the hills and the woods and the farm. I must tell her as we wants a new fence to the chicken run, and that she must bring a child for Mrs. Stanton. And she've got to get busy with Ernie Tucker, so as he don't run away and leave his old pa. And I shall say to them all, to Sid Watson and Tom Grainger and Ted Woolcott and all, I shall turn and say to them: 'Come hither, I will show thee the bride, the Lamb's wife.' But no, she ain't no wife, not the New Year, not yet. She be young and pure and shy, and it be I as must tell her what to do. And the bells do ring out for her, and I be drawing her along in a golden chariot, to sit upon a great white throne. And each tug that I gives to the reins of her chariot do lead her among the fields of stars, as it were one of Farmer Lucas' buttercup fields in May. 214356. 241536. 425136. How they bells do ring. It be like a voice from heaven, as the voice of many waters, singing a new song.' Three at a time, the men rang down the bells. With a smooth, sleek feeling, the ropes rose and fell. Triumphantly, the men swung on to the bell ropes, as they rose for the last time. The silence in the belfry beat down upon them from the stone walls around.

Timothy Childs lurched home. But he did not feel the cold or notice the falling snow. As a god he walked, one who had marshalled time and held within his hands the destiny of the earth. Like a sleep walker he lifted the latch of the garden gate and crossed the path, stumbling against the snow-banked water butt at the back door.

Jane waited for him.

'It's a wild look you've got in your eyes, Tim. It's that fever, I tell you. Here, you come straight to bed, or you'll be hearing they bells in the churchyard next year.'

She pulled him forward, but he jerked himself away from her.

'Don't you dare to touch me – me what have stood in the heavens with the Almighty, tossing the stars about and bringing in the New Year in her golden chariot. Me what have been given the power to. . .'

The figure of the man crumbled, and fell huddled in the chair by the fire.

His power had gone.

Please contact Little Toller Books
to join our mailing list or for more information
on current and forthcoming titles.

Nature Classics Library

IN THE COUNTRY *Kenneth Allsop*
THE JOURNAL OF A DISAPPOINTED MAN *W.N.P. Barbellion*
DOWN THE RIVER *H.E. Bates*
THROUGH THE WOODS *H.E. Bates*
APPLE ACRE *Adrian Bell*
MEN AND THE FIELDS *Adrian Bell*
THE MILITARY ORCHID *Jocelyn Brooke*
THE MIRROR OF THE SEA *Joseph Conrad*
ISLAND YEARS, ISLAND FARM *Frank Fraser Darling*
THE PATTERN UNDER THE PLOUGH *George Ewart Evans*
A TIME FROM THE WORLD *Rowena Farre*
SWEET THAMES RUN SOFTLY *Robert Gibbings*
THE MAKING OF THE ENGLISH LANDSCAPE *W.G. Hoskins*
A SHEPHERD'S LIFE *W.H. Hudson*
WILD LIFE IN A SOUTHERN COUNTY *Richard Jefferies*
BROTHER TO THE OX *Fred Kitchen*
COUNTRY MATTERS *Clare Leighton*
FOUR HEDGES *Clare Leighton*
LETTERS FROM SKOKHOLM *R.M. Lockley*
DREAM ISLAND *R.M. Lockley*
HOME COUNTRY *Richard Mabey*
THE UNOFFICIAL COUNTRYSIDE *Richard Mabey*
RING OF BRIGHT WATER *Gavin Maxwell*
FRESH WOODS, PASTURES NEW *Ian Niall*
EARTH MEMORIES *Llewelyn Powys*
IN PURSUIT OF SPRING *Edward Thomas*
THE SOUTH COUNTRY *Edward Thomas*
THE NATURAL HISTORY OF SELBORNE *Gilbert White*
THE SHINING LEVELS *John Wyatt*

LITTLE TOLLER BOOKS
Lower Dairy, Toller Fratrum, Dorset DT2 0EL.
Telephone: 01300 321536
books@littletoller.co.uk
www.littletoller.co.uk